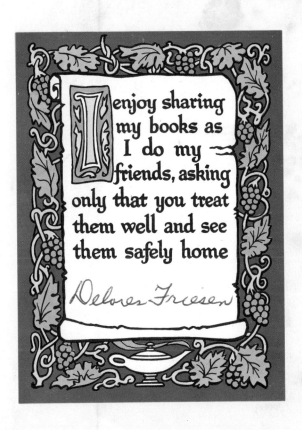

I enjoy sharing my books as I do my friends, asking only that you treat them well and see them safely home

Delores Friesen

THE MEANING OF PERSONS

THE MEANING
OF PERSONS

PAUL TOURNIER

HARPER & ROW, PUBLISHERS

New York and Evanston

Translated by Edwin Hudson from the French
Le Personnage et la Personne, Editions
Delachaux & Niestlé, Neuchâtel and Paris

Library of Congress catalog card number: 57-9885

CONTENTS

Translator's Preface   7

Part One
THE PERSONAGE

1. WHO AM I?   11
2. THIS IMPERSONAL WORLD   28
3. THIS CONTRADICTORY BEING   46

Part Two
LIFE

4. UTOPIA   67
5. THE EXAMPLE OF BIOLOGY   84
6. PSYCHOLOGY AND SPIRIT   102

Part Three
THE PERSON

7. THE DIALOGUE   123
8. THE OBSTACLE   141
9. THE LIVING GOD   159

Part Four
COMMITMENT

10. THE WORLD OF THINGS AND THE WORLD
    OF PERSONS   179
11. TO LIVE IS TO CHOOSE   198
12. NEW LIFE   217
    INDEX   235

5

TRANSLATOR'S PREFACE

THE FIRST of Dr Tournier's books to be published in this country, *A Doctor's Casebook in the Light of the Bible*, has met with a very favourable reception. This is no doubt due to the fact that it has come at a time when searching questions are being asked—not least within the medical profession itself—as to whither certain trends in modern medical thought and practice are leading. Taking his stand uncompromisingly on the biblical revelation, Dr Tournier answered that medicine must treat man and view human life as they truly are if it is not to fail in its function in society. While Dr Tournier's standpoint is not that of the fundamentalist, he claimed that the true view of man and his life is only to be found in the biblical perspective.

In the present volume, which is Dr Tournier's latest book, the author develops further his inquiry into what sort of a creature it is with whom the doctor has to deal; and he does not let us forget that the doctor is himself no different in this respect from his patient. Drawing on his long experience as a practising physician and psychologist he stresses the fundamental importance of the personal relationship between doctor and patient on the one hand, and between God and man on the other. His inquiry has led him to a conception of the human personality which was once much better understood in this country than it is today, and to which he does well to recall us. Shakespeare, though he might not have used the same terms as Dr Tournier does, would have had no difficulty in understanding the distinction he makes between the person and the personage:

> *All the world's a stage*
> *And all the men and women merely players;*
> *They have their exits and their entrances;*
> *And one man in his time plays many parts . . .*

Translator's Preface

It is interesting to note that the word 'personage' had in Shakespeare's day the same meaning as that which Dr Tournier here gives to his *'personnage'*. It is for that reason that I have chosen to retain the cognate in my translation.

EDWIN HUDSON

February 1956

PART ONE

THE PERSONAGE

WHO AM I?

TODAY IS a public holiday in Geneva. It is the anniversary of the *Escalade* of 1602 when, one dark December night, God wonderfully delivered the city from a crafty attempt by the Duke of Savoy to take possession of it.

On this day every year the confectioners' shop-windows are full of little chocolate or nougat cooking-pots in memory of a particularly popular episode of the battle: a certain Dame Royaume, seeing the Savoyards passing beneath her windows, took her cooking-pot off the fire and killed one of them by hurling it at his head.

History or legend? Only last night the announcer on the wireless was replying to an anonymous listener who had asked if the anecdote was authentic. The historians, he said, had studied the problem. Professor Geisendorf had established that there was a real Dame Royaume, and that her famous cooking-pot was mentioned in the will of one of her descendants; but the story was probably a later invention, since the oldest documents concerning the *Escalade* make no mention of it.

So we shall probably never know whether the details of the story were accurate. The same might be said of William Tell, of Christopher Columbus, and of every other great historical figure. Specialists even doubt whether some of them—usually the most popular ones—ever existed at all. Where does the frontier between legend and history lie? All the learning of the experts is powerless to demarcate it exactly.

Tradition and reputation, partisanship and animosity have an almost instantaneous effect on the mental picture we form even of our own contemporaries. And the point is that it is that mental picture which counts, which speaks to our hearts, which acts effectively on us, arousing in us real feelings of admiration or reprobation.

One can go further, and recognize that the same applies to each of us in our own eyes. When we evoke our memories, we can never be quite sure that we have banished all illusion from them, however sincere we are. What we call to mind is not the facts themselves but their appearance, the way in which we saw and felt them. All that we have seen and felt—images and sensations—remains more or less distorted in our memories.

Day after day men and women of all ages and conditions, the healthy as well as the sick, come to see me in order to learn to know themselves better. They tell me the story of their lives. They take great trouble to get the details absolutely right. They are seeking to know the person that they themselves really are, and they feel that everything we are setting out to do together may well be compromised if they are not scrupulously sincere in all they say.

It often happens that at the next consultation they will correct some detail, or add a new one the omission of which might falsify my understanding of the facts. Of course this concern is a legitimate one: there could be no discovery of the person without this desire for complete honesty.

There is, however, one point on which I am able to reassure these inquirers: happily, what matters in this search for the person is not so much historical facts as the way in which we see and feel them. If our memories deceive us, the distortion that they have undergone is by no means accidental; it tells us as much about ourselves as do the facts themselves.

In the same way, we learn as much about humanity from legends as from historical reports. They are a different reality, but a reality nevertheless. Indeed, they are a much more reliable document than the most learned history book. If we wish to understand man it is as important to read the *Iliad*, the *Odyssey*, the *Aeneid*, the *Bhagavad-Gita*, or even Grimm's fairy-tales, as philosophical, sociological, physiological or psychological treatises.

Nothing relies on convention more than the theatre. The play that we see there is in fact a 'play' of personages. And yet one tragedy by Sophocles contains as much authentic truth about humanity as the most accurate biography. The actors are playing a part, and yet it is the human person itself that we apprehend in their gestures and their words, as surely as if we were watching a man living his real life. The very word person owes its origin to the masks worn by the actors to amplify their voices (*sonare . . . per*).

Professor C. G. Jung uses the Latin word *persona* to express not what we mean by the word 'person', but rather 'personage', in the sense in which I shall be using it in this book. These linguistic complications are not fortuitous; they testify to the complexity of the problem I am grappling with: the way in which the personage is inextricably bound up with the person, in spite of the fact that we always tend to think of the role we play as different from what we are in reality.

There was a time when legend, poetry and music counted for more than science in the making of a cultivated man. Doubtless it was a more humane age than ours is. Much of what we know today about man, not only about his body, but about the psychological and sociological laws that govern his life, was unknown. Yet it is probably true to say that man was known better then than now.

One of Pirandello's *Six Characters in Search of an Author* declares that an imaginary being like Sancho Panza is more real than any real man. Sancho Panza has in fact the advantage over you and me of being a finished product. He is all that Cervantes has said of him, but nothing more. I, on the other hand, can speak endlessly of myself, to myself or to someone else, without ever succeeding in giving a complete and truthful picture of myself. There remains in every man, even for himself, something of impenetrable mystery.

Where then is the frontier between what I am and what I can become? Who knows whether tomorrow my reactions to some new event will not reveal an aspect of my person more important than any I have so far discovered? Is not what I shall be capable of tomorrow contained in what I am today?

Even Sancho Panza is not identical for everybody; my idea of him is not the same as yours, or as that of Cervantes. For me he is a personal image which the reading of the Quixote has awakened in me, and which my own mental associations and experiences have also helped to fashion: he is *my* Sancho Panza. He depends therefore on my own person and the history of my own life, on the conscious and unconscious resonances aroused in my mind by Cervantes' story.

The same thing happens with all these people who come to see me, and take so much trouble over their efforts to describe themselves to me with strict accuracy; inevitably I form an image of them which derives as much from myself as from them. If they go and see one of my colleagues he will certainly not see them exactly as I do. And they for their part will not show themselves to him in exactly the same way as they show themselves to me.

The reader will see now why it is that this problem of the person has for twenty years been of such absorbing interest to me. It has a general significance which is of vital importance for all thought and all civilization: what is man? But it also has a particular significance, which is equally important for my own life: who am I, really, myself?

It is a question which haunts each one of us, whether we are aware of it or not. It is there in every consultation I give. It is there for the man who comes to see me, and for me as well. This frank and living contact with people is the very substance of my professional life. It is for me, quite as much as for the man who consults me, a means of discovering myself. I seek to attain it not only in my consulting-room, but all the time, in every meeting with another person, in my own family, with my friends, in conferences, and on holiday.

But the man who comes to consult me is asking himself the question more urgently: he wants to understand himself. He expects me to help him. Experience has shown me that this absorbing problem of the person is much more complicated than is commonly thought. It is in order to throw light on some of its aspects that I am writing this book. For me, to write is to converse with my readers, known and unknown. It is to raise with them questions which are raised for me by my own contact with life.

In a manner of speaking I occupy a privileged observation-post. The majority of those who come to see me have made up their minds to reveal themselves to me more openly than they have ever revealed themselves before. They tell me things they have never dared to say to anyone else. It is not just them that I must try to discover, but the human person in each of them, shorn of the deceptive appearances under which it so easily masquerades in everyday life.

And yet, however privileged my observation-post, I become increasingly aware that the person, pure and unvarnished, will always escape us. Doubtless only God knows it. I can never grasp the true reality, of myself or of anybody else, but only an image; a fragmentary and deformed image, an appearance: the 'personage'.

The message, therefore, of this book is what I discover, what seems to me to throw light on the problem of man, and at the same time what always eludes discovery, what remains mysterious and obscure. There is thus a strange relationship between the personage and the person; they are linked together, and yet they remain distinct. I can approach the person only through that image which at one and the same time allows me glimpses of it and also tends to hide it from me, reveals as well as conceals it.

And then man is not static, but living; each consultation gives me a fresh image of him. An undemonstrable yet indisputable intuition tells me that there is unity and continuity in him, even though the successive images seem discontinuous, diverse and even contradictory. An urge towards synthesis impels me to seek the common factor in them, to pass from the lantern slide to the cinematograph film, to comprehend man in his incessant movement.

But the motion picture creates even more illusions than the

separate images. Nothing is more dangerous than to flatter one-self that one has arrived at the synthesis of a life: it can never be more than a diagram, which cuts out all the infinite diversity of life, reducing it to an arbitrary abstraction. I should not have grasped the person, but just one more image, an even more misleading one; an elaboration of my own mind, personal to myself: neither Dame Royaume nor Sancho Panza themselves, but their personages as I see and distort them.

One thing, therefore, that this absorbing search for the person has done is to make me much more cautious over jumping to conclusions. It has made me see how superficial and false are the judgments that people are constantly making about each other. I do not refer only to moral judgments, but to psychological and philosophical judgments as well. Because people reveal them-selves to me more openly, I can see them more clearly than others do. At the same time I am all the more acutely conscious of how far removed from reality my own vision is.

A couple at odds with one another come and consult me. While the husband is talking to me about his wife, I think what he would have said about her when they first became engaged. She may very well have changed since then, but in all probability not as much as her husband thinks.

He had seen her with the eyes of love; he had formed an ideal-ized image of her, and it was this image he loved, believing it to be the reality. Since then he has been hurt again and again, but he is just as biassed: the image he repels and condemns is no more his wife than the other was. I should like to ask him: 'would you not like to get to know your wife?' But the very judgment he passes on her prevents him from really getting to know her.

I was three months old when my father died, so that I know him only from the biography written by one of his friends, from obituary notices, from the poems he left, from articles, letters, photographs, and from stories about him, told me long after-wards. From all this material my mind has built up an image. Inevitably this image depends also on my own psychological

complexes; I have projected my own ideal into it; I have fashioned
—and distorted—it, to make it what I want it to be.

And yet, when a man describes to me his father—a father with
whom he spent his whole childhood, I cannot be sure that the
portrait he paints is any more faithful than the one I have of
mine.

I take up my pen again, and today happens to be another
patriotic festival. The reader will be thinking that we have them
quite often in Geneva! It is the anniversary of the Restoration
of the Republic, when the Austrians came and freed us from
the French occupation, on the 31st December, 1813.

At dawn this morning the cannon boomed on the ramparts.
Every year I go up there and meet patriotic citizens who still
exchange the old greeting: 'Long live Austria! Long live the
Republic!' The children, stopping their ears near the guns, are
there too, taken by their elders to be initiated into the traditions
of their city and the love of their country.

I have just been to a commemoration service in the cathedral,
where a packed congregation gave thanks to God, the
protector of the city, and listened to the story of the historical
events, and the Church's exhortations to authorities and
citizens.

As a Genevan, all this means a great deal to me. The echoes of a
thousand childhood memories, indelibly printed on my mind,
are aroused by the day's events. There is something here that is
peculiar to the little country in which I was born, a country
whose political life has always been closely bound up with its
spiritual destiny.

And yet a critical onlooker might well describe it all as a
conventional stage-setting, with its personages—those members
of the government sitting solemnly in their stalls, aware of the
furtive glances cast in their direction by the crowd; all those
people comporting themselves as they feel befits a great occasion;
the preacher in his pulpit, with his exaggerated gestures and his
voice carefully pitched. He takes care not to be too solemn,

but at the same time his hearers would not be satisfied were he to speak to them as if he were chatting to them in the street.

Suddenly, amid the hushed silence of the nave, a child's voice is heard:

'Daddy! Daddy! Who's that man talking up there?'

Doubtless it is the first time he has been brought to church. He has not been trained in the social conventions yet. His father is very embarrassed, and instead of answering his quite natural question whispers to him to be quiet. But around me I catch one or two smiles, as if the child's spontaneity had in some way brought a welcome relief, as if a window had been opened, and fresh air allowed to blow where the weight of solemnity was beginning to be rather stifling.

I have often had occasion in my consulting-room to listen to a man who was full of complaints against society, bitterly denouncing the hollow vanity of all civic and religious ceremonies. What a lot of drivel an intelligent man can talk in front of an applauding crowd! When a man rejects the claims of society he soon comes to feel that public ceremonial is just a sinister comedy, that the whole thing is artificial—a stage-setting carefully arranged beforehand, in which everybody, orators, officials and audience, are acting a part. With revolutionaries the stage-setting is different, but it is a stage-setting nevertheless.

My patient would protest in the name of the life that is being crushed by society. Is not life spontaneity, sincerity, authenticity? There is no trace of that in these official personages. They are no longer men, but merely puppets worked by some anonymous stage-manager pulling the strings behind the scenes.

There was nothing I could say in reply. It is all true. I understood the complaint all the better when the person who made it had told me the story of his life. As with every man, myself included, the key to his ideas lay in the circumstances of his own personal existence. His parents had been slaves to the idea of 'What will people say?' He would have liked to go and play in the street with comrades who seemed to him to be marvellous people, and to dress as they dressed. He had been forbidden to do so:

'Boys of our class don't roam the streets in company with urchins.'

His brother, on the other hand, had all the tastes his parents approved of. He was a good little boy who always brought home glowing reports from school. My patient soon realized that his parents preferred his brother to him; the brother was a credit to them, whereas he put them to shame.

'It's just one worry after another with you,' they would say to him. 'You'll never make anything of your life! If only you would follow your brother's example!'

He grew to detest his brother, now a personage of some importance in public life. He saw him as the incarnation of a family and social conformity that revolted him.

That man's story is passing through my mind as the ceremony proceeds. Doubtless, if I had undergone the same fate I too should be in revolt against society. The circumstances of my life have been quite different: but they have no less influence on the way I look at things. In a few minutes, when I leave here, I shall shake hands with old friends; others, less intimately acquainted, will make some sign, and touch their hats. I am a doctor, a writer. Apparently I enjoy the esteem of my fellow-citizens. I too am necessarily a personage.

Occasionally someone stops me to say how interesting he has found my latest book. Flattering, is it not? Someone else criticizes my ideas; that is flattering too. This society which repels the rebel, or worse still, ignores him, forces me to play its game in spite of all that I know about human vanity and my own vanity. And even if I take a stand against convention, I shall be thought original and courageous; in the rebel it would be termed impertinence.

Deep inside me I feel more sympathy for this rebel, in spite of all his misdeeds, than for his brother who is perhaps sitting over there in the cathedral stalls. I am a servant of Jesus Christ. He stood out against the powerful formalism of his day. He made friends with those who had no part with the great personages whom he reproved for taking the highest seats at a banquet. The latter never forgave him for it, and they had him nailed to a cross.

And yet I must admit that my life is less like that of the rebel than that of his brother. Although in my consulting-room I enter into fellowship with the former, here I am with the latter, amid all these people who share in a traditional social order. And because there is a certain accord between these people and me I am able to see something else which the rebel does not see. In this stage-setting, which to him is a mere masquerade, I see the reflection, the concrete expression, of an invisible but living reality. My country is also a person, arrayed in the finery of tradition. That is the reality which this crowd is seeking. Behind the official personages, behind the ritual gestures whose very repetition confers upon them a physiognomy which we come to know and love, there is indeed a person which draws us to itself. Patriotism is a personal communion with one's fatherland.

Every person has a face. So also has one's fatherland, though to some it seems to be only a mask. I cannot love it in the abstract—I must love it as I see it: the poetry of its countryside, its lake and its hills; its far-off mountains; its cathedral, celebrated in verse by my father; the whole of its past, the heroes of the *Escalade*, the citizens of the Restoration, and all the personages of its history—Calvin, Jean-Jacques Rousseau, General Dufour who brought peace to my homeland, and Henri Dunant the founder of the Red Cross.

Beyond my town is my country, William Tell, Nicolas de Flue, its writers and artists, the beacons lit on the mountain-tops on the night of the National Festival, the gay songs of the Tessin, the majesty of the Grisons, the narrow fastness of the Grutli, the ramparts of Morat, the vineyards of Lake Leman. My country's scenery, the setting of my own existence. A setting only? Of course—and yet without it I should not be what I am; all these things have gone to make me the sort of person I am. My person depends and is projected on them.

I see well enough also that it is impossible to understand a Frenchman, a Finn, a Greek or an American without putting him in the context of the scenery of his life, the history of his people, the background of his family, his job, his festivals and his customs. This man who comes into my study speaks to me not only through the words he utters. His face, chubby or hollow-cheeked, his hands, slender or stubby, his appearance, well-groomed or Bohemian, the way he sits down or shakes hands, the character he has given to his home, the wife he has chosen, the children he pets or scolds, everything that goes to make up his personage, even what he purposely adds to it either from guile or from vanity—all is equally indicative of his person for one who is in search of the person.

We have come back to our starting point. How can we discover the true person when we see only distorted and varied images of it, and when these images derive their origin not only from the man himself, but also from ourselves, and from the whole environment to which he belongs? It is no use trying to arrive at an exact picture by adding all the many false images together. That would be like trying to get a complete picture of an individual by superimposing hundreds of different negatives of him on one photographic print. Synthesis is not addition.

Nevertheless it is my daily experience that this search for the true person is not fruitless. In front of me sits a man. He has told me much about his life and about himself, with that concern for complete honesty that I mentioned earlier. I have myself paid attention to the smallest details, for they all have their importance.

'I admire your patience', he tells me, 'listening to all this, when much of it must seem to you pointless.'

The remark astonishes me. To call it patience is to suppose an effort on my part, whereas the truth is that it is far more interesting to understand one man thoroughly than to examine a hundred superficially.

But it is not the registering of these details that counts, important though they be. I could go on accumulating notes and observations, but they would not reveal the person to me. Nevertheless, assisted by this apparently objective inquiry, something of a quite different order takes place, almost without our being aware of it. There is established between us a bond of sympathy and affection, the fruit, in fact, of our sincerity the one towards the other.

There suddenly awakens within me the certainty that I am no longer learning, but understanding. It is quite different. It is not the sum of what I have learnt. It is a light which has suddenly burst forth from our personal contact. That man could go on endlessly revealing facts about himself, but the light would never shine out unless we found this contact. And, further, nothing he can tell me now will ever be able to veil it.

A characteristic feature is that he has experienced this inner certainty at the same time as I. He felt that he was understood. More than that: he felt also that he was understanding himself better, and that I was understanding him just as he understood himself. We become fully conscious only of what we are able to express to someone else. We may already have had a certain inner intuition about it, but it must remain vague so long as it is un-formulated. In that moment our two persons have met. Personal contact has been made. It is as if I had discovered him, not now from without, but from within.

From all that I had learnt about him up to this moment I might have been able to sketch a picture of his temperament, his character, his personality: 'a portrait', as the graphologists say. From what I know of psychology I might have interpreted the picture, and worked out an explanation of the man's behaviour. If I were a Freudian I should explain it in terms of the interplay of his instincts and the social resistances they have encountered. Were I a Jungian, I should explain it in terms of the processes of individuation and integration. If I were a disciple of Adler, of Pavlov, or of any other psychologist, I should find in this same picture material illustrative of the particular theories I had adopted.

In fact, I refuse to consider these various doctrines mutually exclusive. I am fully persuaded that they all have something interesting, true and useful to contribute to the understanding of people. But they explain only mechanisms of the mind. Similarly, the study of all the physiological mechanisms of the body can never of itself lead us to a knowledge of the person. All that is mechanical in man, every physical or psychical phenomenon, is of the order of the personage, and not of the person.

It is precisely because objective scientific disciplines are in-involved that we are able to form a picture; a picture which, in spite of our efforts to be objective, depends, as we have seen, upon our own particular theories to which we relate the indefinable moving flux of life, in an attempt to systematize it so that we can study it. It is a study, an explanation, an interpretation, not an understanding. That is proved by the fact that there are as many true and interesting interpretations as there are psychological doctrines.

The intuitive understanding which I have just described, the personal contact which my patient and I both experienced at once and which awakened in us the certainty that we understood each other, seems at first sight to be much more subjective, since it is no longer scientific. And that is why it is much more independent of whatever psychological theories each of us may have.

A Freudian or a Jungian will experience just as I do this sudden personal contact with his patient. All that he has done with the patient hitherto, employing his own scientific techniques, will have contributed towards its taking place, just as in my case the long approach I have described has also prepared the way. And it is clear that in dealing with sick people a more rigorous technique than mine may well be indispensable.

The apprehension of the person, then, seems to me to be not one more explanatory theory, but a fact of a new and different order. It does not depend upon the images of a man which we may form for ourselves, each according to his own particular theories, nor upon the historical accuracy of what he tells us. A factor common to all psychological techniques is that desire for sincerity which, as we have seen, is the essential prerequisite of personal contact.

I was made acutely aware of this on one occasion some time ago. A woman was relating to me an episode which she regarded as the most painful of her childhood. A moment before, she had confessed her doubts of the matter:

'I am afraid of misleading you', she had said, 'if I describe what I then experienced as I felt it at the time. I was only a child, and doubtless I did not see things as they really were, so that you perhaps will be led to pass an unfair judgment on my mother.'

I had reassured her on the point. A doctor's consulting-room is neither a magistrate's court nor a historian's study. If I am to understand this woman she must express what she felt. If I wanted to understand her mother, I ought to be listening to her mother. I am too well aware of how different my idea of her would then be, to pass judgment on her on the basis of the things her daughter says.

But this woman was still in the grip of a profound emotion, a concern for the truth that amounted to an obsession. She spoke very slowly, taking infinite pains to find the right word. Then suddenly I found myself trembling inwardly. 'Here is a heart that is trying to be absolutely truthful', I thought, 'what a majestic thing it is!' I felt as if I were confronted by something supernatural, something that overwhelmed me.

I was very far from judging her mother! Historical truth is the object of intellectual knowledge and judgment. Here we were dealing with something quite different. But the extreme concern for truth which filled this woman's mind was opening the door to a truth of a new order, a truth which is outside history and time, a truth in its own right. And that is what I call understanding.

This it is which has healing and human value. Intellectual understanding will suffice for the writing of an individual's life-history; such an account must, as we have observed, always be treated with reserve. An understanding of its psychological mechanisms will suffice for the formulation of a particular interpretation—possibly very penetrating—of an individual's mind. But at the moment of true understanding there takes place an event which is not to be defined intellectually, whether by historical or by psychological description.

I may forget many of the facts that that woman had told me. But that trembling that went through me I shall not forget. What happened at that moment was that I passed from information to communion. Information is intellectual, whereas communion is spiritual; but information was the path that led to communion. Information speaks of personages. Communion touches the person. Through information I can understand a case; only through communion shall I be able to understand a person. Men expect of us that we should understand them as cases; but they also want to be understood as persons.

There are then two routes to be followed in the knowledge of man: one is objective and scientific, the other is subjective and intuitive. They cannot be equated together, for they require the exercise of utterly different faculties. One proceeds by logical analysis and precise assessment; the other by a total understanding. One is an endless progression; the other is a sudden and complete discovery.

The two roads do cross, however. Objective exploration prepares the way for the personal encounter, as we have just seen. Conversely, the personal encounter opens the road for more penetrating objective observation. Such is my daily experience, as it is also of those of my colleagues who claim that they are confining themselves strictly to the scientific point of view, though it is a fact they may not always admit. The personal communion which is established between them and their patients removes psychological 'censorship' in the latter, so opening the door to a profounder study of their psychical mechanisms.

One of my patients dreamed that she had to come and see me, and was looking for her Sunday dress but could not find it. Then, still in the dream, she realized that she did not have to wear her Sunday dress in order to come and see me. This was a symbol of liberation from the personage: she feels at ease with me now, because communion has been established; she can show herself as she is, instead of acting a part as she must do in everyday life.

However, although the two methods—that of intellectual information and that of spiritual communion—are thus mutually supporting, it is not easy to synthesize them. Our minds do not seem readily able to comprehend man at once as an ensemble of phenomena and as a person. If we concentrate on the phenomena, the person escapes us; if we see the person, the phenomena become blurred.

There was a great deal of discussion during the nineteenth century on the subject of determinism and free will: and at that time almost the only determinism known was the physico-chemical and the physiological. Since then the scientific picture of man has been completed; the circle of rigorous determinism has been closed, for the work done by the psychoanalysts, by the followers of Pavlov, and by modern sociologists, has given us a picture of man determined not only in his body, but in every feeling and thought as well. According to Jean Rostand, 'man is but an automaton in movement'.[1]

Discussions on this theme have taken place at Zurich, under the chairmanship of Professor Ferdinand ·Gonseth.[2] One after another the mathematician, the physicist, the physiologist and the psychologist came forward to describe the view of the world and of man to which science is bringing us: that of a 'causal explanation' which allows no place for chance or for liberty. But suddenly a new voice makes itself heard in the debate—that of the 'individualist', who intuitively protests: 'The picture of the human being that we can accept with enthusiasm is certainly not that of a perfect automaton. My protest is total and unqualified: I am alive.' And the philosopher adds: 'Here we have an experience which cannot be reduced to a causal explanation.'

An experience—it is true that life, the person, liberty, personal

[1] Jean Rostand, *La vie et ses problèmes*, Flammarion, Paris, 1939.
[2] See his book *Déterminisme et libre arbitre*, Editions du Griffon, Neuchâtel, 1944.

commitment and communion are not unfolding phenomena, but an experience which compels total and unqualified recognition. One of the dangers of an age which puts a premium on science and technology is that doctors may lose this sense of the person. It is especially as he approaches death, which Dr Troisfontaines has justly described[1] as the 'strictly personal' experience *par excellence*, that the patient needs to be seen by his doctor not as an automaton, but as a person.

[1] R. Troisfontaines, 'La mort, épreuve de l'amour, condition de la liberté,' in *La mort*, Centre d'études Laennec, Paris, 1948.

2

THIS IMPERSONAL WORLD

'I HAVE COME to see you because I am looking for life!'
The visitor who greets me with these words is a man about
whom the most striking thing is the friendliness that seems to
radiate from his face.

He explains to me that he has just come from the house of a
friend who represents his country in the United Nations Organization. A brilliant reception was in progress there, and the house
was thronging with all the important international figures of
Geneva. He gives me a vivid and penetrating description of it.
Behind the bowing and the smiles, behind the friendly words, the
witticisms, the empty phrases, and even in their silences and their
aloofness, all were playing a cautious game. Each sought to dis-
semble his own real thoughts, his secret intentions, while trying
to unmask those of his neighbour.

It was not only a matter of diplomatic intrigues; there were
sentimental manœuvres going on too, and those subtle tactics in
which we all constantly indulge in order to consolidate our
prestige and give to others the desired impression. These various
purposes combined and interacted as each pursued his own
ends.

Everything was studied—dress, jewels, handshake, the subject
of conversation. The servants played their part with a proper
impassibility. The hosts displayed all the attentiveness demanded
by the occasion. All these people meet together frequently in
various fashionable drawing-rooms, and the game goes on and
develops. Among them all exists a tacit understanding which they
scrupulously observe.

'What a farce!' exclaims my visitor, But he is able to denounce
it so lucidly because he himself is conscious of the fact that he is

constantly acting a part, as much to himself as to others; he suffers from it to the point of obsession.

'I'm looking for life!' And he adds: 'I am not living a real life at all.'

The agony of it has pursued him everywhere year after year. There is nothing in all that but a façade, a caricature, a mere appearance of life. His memories pour out, full of that agonizing impression of meeting, not men, but more or less artificial personages, and the worse agony of feeling that he is himself caught up in the game, so that he can never be spontaneous, simple and true.

'Only on rare occasions have I succeeded', he says; 'when I have been in love. And even then the spell was broken almost at once, because I realized that it was not really love I was looking for, but life; love was just one more pretence. And in order to keep even that, my words and attitudes had to be carefully calculated; I had to play the game of love in the way the woman expected me to; to give way to her whims in order to please her; or else she had to follow mine, in order not to lose me. And so life escapes us just when we think it is in our grasp.'

Suddenly he breaks off. 'You're making me feel nervous,' he says to me.

'How do you mean?'

'Yes, you are. For the last moment or two I have been saying just anything—anything but what I wanted to say to you.'

What feeling had I momentarily experienced? It was probably quite unconscious, because I was full of sympathy for that man in his search for life, and deeply interested in what he was saying. Perhaps the very fact that he was able to express so well things that I too am aware of had caused some subtle movement of envy in me.

In any case, with his quick intuition he had sensed the breaking of that personal contact of which we were speaking just now, and which is the prerequisite of life, spontaneity and communion. But the contact was re-established from the moment he had the courage to tell me I was making him nervous. How fragile a thing we see that genuine fellowship to be! For in ordinary life it is impossible always to be laying bare one's heart. One has to enclose it in protective armour.

A foreign colleague remarked to me recently that he was in the habit of taking part in meetings for 'collective psychoanalysis', where, he said, the strict rule is that everybody must say exactly what he thinks, without any pretence or keeping anything back. I confess I burst out laughing. That was naughty of me, for those people are undoubtedly sincere, and believe that they do keep their rule. But I am very much afraid that, all trained in the same school of psychoanalysis, they unwittingly remain subject to a tacit convention of some kind. Psychoanalysis has liberated them from certain social conventions, but inevitably it has created new ones. Every society and every movement eventually acquires its own particular vocabulary and code of behaviour. One does not notice it if one is on the inside; it is those outside who see it. Every army has its uniform. Even the language we speak inescapably moulds the way we express ourselves.

Courtesy and restraint hold sway in social life, which would be impossible without them. I need only think of the first words I should utter were I to join that society of psychoanalysts, and wished to follow their rules, in order to realize how wicked, susceptible, impure, proud and dishonest I am. Outside close intimacy and the miracle of the presence of God, real honesty seems to me to be utopian.

But which of us is free of the torment my visitor disclosed to me? If we open our eyes upon those around us and upon ourselves, we see the game in which all, without exception, are engaged. Each plays what trumps he has to gain his own altruistic or egotistical ends. We are like chess-players scheming to win our game; or rather each of us lives his life like those chess-masters who play a hundred games simultaneously.

Whatever our aim—the conquest of a woman, of money, pleasure, esteem or notoriety, the defence of ourselves or our loved ones, or even of our opinions and our faith—moment by moment our attitudes and our words are governed by it and our

personage moulded by it. It happens in every office, in every factory, in every society, in every committee, and even within the family circle. The assertive ones use the weapon of intimidation; others play on the heart-strings, or resort to cunning. Alliances are formed and dissolved, plans for revenge are made. A witty reply affords a way of escape; what we say very often serves less to express an opinion than to win a point or to justify ourselves.

I was very impressed the other day by a man who was telling me of the decisive moment in his life when he found that true life which my other visitor was looking for. Torn in early youth by the war from a life of wealth and ease, and hunted by the Nazis, who had invaded his country, he was destitute and in flight at the time. In the street he saw an itinerant vendor selling buns, but he had no money with which to buy any. A wretched beggar came up and bought himself one, and then, turning and seeing him standing there, offered it to him instead of eating it himself.

That simple, spontaneous gesture overwhelmed the young man. It was a complete revelation to him; it made a different man of him. And ever since that day he, like my other visitor, has been tormented by the continual camouflage in which civilized society indulges.

'I cannot board a trolley-bus', he told me, 'without feeling an urge to offer up a silent prayer at the sight of all those people packed together, eyeing each other, judging each other by appearances, calculating their chances and trying to keep themselves in countenance.'

Thus the whole of social life is like a game, in every sense of the word. Firstly in the sense of an amusement, for in many respects it is a 'diversion', in Pascal's sense, in which men seek to escape from their personal distress. We ought frankly to admit that we allow ourselves to be drawn into the game, that we are even pleased to join in, and that it hurts us to feel ourselves strangers to a community, excluded from its game.

A closely related meaning of the word is that of competitive sport. Take the example of an industrialist whose health is not very robust, a fact which is a great worry to him. He is always feeling at the end of his tether; when he comes back from a business trip or from his office he is so tired that he has to go and lie down, and as a result his family life is greatly restricted. He has, however, a sense of the value of human relationships. He recognizes that the bigger his organization grows, the less personal contact he can have with his colleagues. But this has not prevented him from considerably enlarging the industrial undertaking he directs, over the last few years. He is still zealously working to expand it.

Connected with the idea of playing a game is a different kind of play, that of the stage. Life is like a drama in which each of us has his part to play; the footlights are on, the curtain up: none of us can drop out without compromising the success of his fellows. Then again, game signifies convention: we speak of 'playing the game'. The 'rules of the game' are a powerful convention to which we all bow, including the non-conformist, for he provides an exception provided for and neutralized in advance. And lastly there is the idea of slavery, the slavery of the gambler who cannot tear himself from the game which has become his vice.

We are the slaves of the personage which we have invented for ourselves or which has been imposed on us by others. Jean-Paul Sartre[1] has some penetrating things to say on the subject. An inkstand is of itself an inkstand, and nothing else; whereas to Sartre a man is always 'in representation'. A restaurant-waiter is only a restaurant-waiter on condition that he plays the part of a restaurant-waiter, with all the gestures and behaviour proper to such a role. I am reminded of Dr Allendy's *Journal d'un médecin malade*,[2] where with awful lucidity he describes the colleagues and friends who came to see him during his last illness. Behind every word and attitude he is able to distinguish

[1] See Gabriel Marcel, 'L'existence et la liberté humaine chez Jean-Paul Sartre', in *Les grands appels de l'homme contemporain*, Editions du Temps présent, Paris, 1946.

[2] René Allendy, *Journal d'un médecin malade*, Denoël, Paris, 1944.

that secret and incessant defence of oneself and of one's reputation, sometimes conscious, sometimes unconscious. 'We strive continually', wrote Pascal, 'to adorn and preserve our imaginary self, neglecting the true one.'

Even if we would, we could not escape this constant make-believe. Not only is it imposed on us from without by the necessities of social life: it has become a second nature. Our personage clings to our person by dint of a long schooling which has made us what we are. It starts in the first few days of our life; it becomes more intensive when we go to school, for school is a mould designed to standardize the human material poured into it. The child who shows originality and refuses to submit to the process is regarded as a black sheep, and thereafter he will play that role just as his classmate will play the role of the good little boy.

Each generation of pupils passes on to the next its store of 'tips' on how to answer the various masters in the examinations; for the aim is not to give vent to personal views, but to obtain the examination certificates which are the passport into a place in society. Later we learn the sort of behaviour which will win us acceptance among our workmates, the esteem of our chief, the respect of our rivals, the appreciation of our clients, and which will hold at arm's length those whose company would harm us, while helping us to associate with those who are useful to us.

The whole of our education, our titles, honours and decorations, our daily experience of life, our relationships, friendships, relatives, possessions, all go to make up our personage; they impart to it its peculiar physiognomy, and either consolidate or compromise our relations with everyone we meet. We have learned our lesson so well that it becomes as spontaneous as a new instinct. In order to see the unadulterated self it would be necessary to strip off all these accretions. But that is an illusion: if I burnt my diploma it would not stop anyone thinking of me as Dr Tournier. If I burnt all my books, I should still be the man who wrote them.

There are in addition all the attributes, both good and bad, that we have in other people's eyes. We are inevitably influenced

33

by them. Take the case of a man who, when over thirty years old, discovered in the intimacy of a journey taken with him what sort of a person his father really was. Until then he had regarded him as the typical 'heavy-handed father', and had been terrified of him.

'If you don't behave yourself', his mother always used to say to him, 'I'll tell your father!'

And the father, in spite of himself and in spite of all the affection he had for his child, played the role of bogy man.

In this way the mutual relationships of the members of every family are crystallized. I see it clearly when one of my patients, after treatment, comes to know himself better, and acquires a new freedom in his behaviour. Nearly always he finds himself encountering strong resistance, because he is disturbing the established order; and the family is quick to think that I have a bad influence on him. When they entrusted him to me they had not reckoned with this unexpected consequence. There arise conflicts which were unknown before.

There was the girl who played the role of Cinderella in her family. She always stayed at home to help her mother with the housework while her sisters used to go out. She suddenly announces that she has been invited out for the evening. Everybody expostulates, 'You can't got out tonight; you know very well that your sister has to go to a club meeting; you might think about her a little instead of being so selfish.'

Even between husband and wife it requires a miracle to establish, and still more, to maintain, complete frankness. The fear of being misunderstood, of being criticized, judged, even despised, keeps back certain confessions and confidences. The reactions of the one soon lead the other to humour him in certain matters, to adopt a behaviour that will avoid difficulties. Of course it is quite right to make mutual concessions. But it is one thing to do it freely, and to have the courage to speak openly about it, and quite another to adopt unwillingly an artificial attitude.

There takes place particularly between husband and wife a sort of formation by contrast, which I have noted elsewhere. The more loquacious the one is, the more silent the other, and the more the first talks in order to fill the silence. The more cautious and timid the one, the more the other affects boldness and daring. The more severe one is with the children, the more the other is inclined to grant them clandestine favours. The more thrifty the one, the more extravagant the other. The first, in order to set an example, imposes excessive restrictions on his natural inclinations. Just think what would happen if he were to admit that he would like to make such and such a purchase! What an encouragment to the dangerous propensities of his wife!

So each accentuates his own tendencies in order to counterbalance those of the other. Each acts his part and becomes its prisoner. Each, in the privacy of my consulting-room, confesses that he or she is very different from what the partner imagines. The life of many families is stifled because they have gradually become petrified in stereotyped and extraordinarily powerful habits. The same old discussion crops up regularly on the same old subject, and the same old arguments are trotted out. If the husband should chance one day to make an appreciative remark about some dish, his wife will give him it over and over again. and announce to all and sundry that it is the only thing he likes.

I once heard Dr Théodore Bovet, a specialist in marital problems, remark that the worst enemy of marriage was plain boredom. It is true that boredom inevitably creeps in when the subtle fluidity of the person insensibly coagulates in a personage. Even sexual life can lose its whimsical fantasy and congeal into conventional ritual.

A colleague for whom I have the highest regard once sent me a woman patient together with a friendly note of explanation. Weeks passed, but in spite of good will on both sides our consultations seemed to be bearing no fruit. Then I prayed about it, and it was borne in upon me that the obstacle was in me: I was concerning myself too much with being successful, in order to prove myself worthy of the confidence my colleague had shown in me.

For since I hold him in very high esteem, naturally I value the regard he has for me, and I do not wish to disappoint him.

That very day I spoke of this to my patient, and the atmosphere of our consultations changed completely. My fear of failure had made me less natural. That made failure more likely, and so the vicious circle was closed. I was becoming a personage; I wanted to play a successful role—for the good of my patient, certainly, but also in order to come up to the expectations I supposed my colleague to have of me. We are touching here on a most difficult problem, that of our desire to appear in a favourable light.

Our personage is fashioned not only by our instincts, our egoisms and our vanities, but also by our legitimate ambitions, even those which seem most disinterested. We are flattered when people expect our help; and I confess that I am never insensible of that particular form of flattery. A patient has formed his own idea of me long before he comes to see me. I remember one man who was unable to conceal his surprise when I opened the waiting-room door. He told me that he had pictured me as an old man with a white beard.

I have no intention of growing a beard, and should in any case be unable to turn it prematurely white. But I am sure my readers understand the subtle temptation which always assails me: that of trying to be the personage I am expected to be. It slips in disguised as an honest concern for the proper fulfilment of my vocation. That man who is looking for life—how much I should like to offer him it on a plate! He may possibly undergo some decisive experience while under my care. But the point is that that will certainly not happen if I try to provoke it, for example by looking for something telling to say to him. What is genuinely living cannot be called forth to order; it springs up without our knowing how.

Mine is a wonderful vocation: helping people to discover themselves, to solve the problems of their lives. But it can easily become a mere 'job', a 'business' of personal contact, of humanity, of love. I am so keenly conscious of the danger that I am paralysed, as it were, if I feel that my patient looks upon it like that, expecting some 'trick of the trade', some technique or procedure in which he imagines me to be a past master. If it is given to me to make this personal contact with people, it is precisely because I do not find it easy, for by nature and psychological make-up I am reserved, timid and unsociable; and because I must ask God daily to liberate me from myself so that I may be put at the disposal of others.

Further, I have a threefold vocation: medical, psychological and spiritual. It is bad enough to fall into a technical routine as a doctor or as a psychologist; it is much worse to turn soul-healing into a matter of routine. I confess that it is this spiritual vocation which interests me most, for the very reason that all my experience has taught me the limitations of medicine and of psychology, and because the supreme and universal need of men is to find God.

Many people realize this, and that is why they come to see me. They sometimes say to me: 'Ah! I wish I had a steadfast faith like yours!'

In order not to disappoint them I ought to tell them only of my positive experiences. In fact they are always disconcerted at first, when I speak of my own difficulties, doubts and failings. But they soon come to see that this atmosphere of truth brings us closer and binds us together. My experience of the power of God means more to them than it would if they thought me a quite different sort of person from themselves.

But though I may speak in private of my own troubles, it is clear that greater reserve is required in public. The preacher in his pulpit, even during the gloomy periods of his personal life, must proclaim a message of faith with a constancy unaffected by the ups and downs of his own spiritual life.

The vocation of the minister of religion is no more exempt than any other from the danger of professionalism. The daughter of a pastor once brought me a letter she had had from her father. He had written to her as he might to one of his parishioners. It was a beautiful letter—much too beautiful. She had heard those exhortations so often that they were no longer capable of finding their mark. Seeing an old retired pastor one day, a tram conductor remarked: 'He always had a word of greeting for us before he retired.'

All this is inevitable, and many believers are worried by it. I even think it to be one of the hidden causes of the tension one often feels in the councils of the Church and on the committees of religious organizations. I have seen many men coming away from such meetings full of a vague uneasiness—and after a few years they have grown discouraged, and have resigned. It is not possible for people to work together at a common task without there being differences of opinion, conflicts, jealousy and bitterness. And in a religious organization they are less willing to bring these differences out into the open. They feel quite sincerely that as Christians they ought to be showing a spirit of forgiveness, charity and mutual support. The aggressiveness is repressed, taking the form of anxiety.

I should like with all my heart to be full of love for all my patients, for I know well that that is what they need most, and what Jesus Christ expects of me. I cannot escape the danger of trying to show it when I have not got it, of covering up criticism and irritation under a mask of amiability, the discordance of which an intuitive person is quick to note. Is this then the price that has to be paid in every noble vocation? *Noblesse oblige*, after all. The master must hide from his pupils the gaps in his knowledge. The barrister must show himself confident of success. The doctor would do grave harm to the morale of his patient were he to impart to him all his doubts about his diagnosis and prognosis. The university professor would not be considered a serious scholar unless he published a large number of books.

Sometimes we pretend to be in a hurry; at other times we act as if we had all the time in the world, in spite of our impatience. We do not dare to refuse to make a gift, because a certain person has asked us. We have our secret vanities which are much more naïve. I remember, shortly before receiving my doctorate, practising the new signature which I hoped soon to put into use, a complicated and artificial flourish which I soon abandoned.

As for that diplomatic game which my foreign visitor was describing, we have to admit that we find exactly the same thing in any learned or philanthropic gathering. A medical conference, an academic meeting, a society of artists, a sports committee, all necessarily present the same picture of as many conflicting tendencies as there are individuals, each concerned to make the most of his own part in the work, his own experience, and the original ideas he has had. One cannot spend years working for an organization without identifying oneself with it and scheming to defend it. Between the diplomat serving his country and the chairman of a committee, the trade union secretary or the adherent of a religious sect, there is not much difference. That is why it is easier to found a society or a movement than to suppress it or to merge it into another.

If the purpose of the society is praiseworthy and useful, then concern for its welfare seems all the more legitimate. I am reminded of the experience of a woman who decided to join a certain religious community. She had been attracted by the care its members had shown for her, and the interest they had taken in her as a person—which she had badly needed at the time. But when she had donned its uniform she realized that what was required of her, quite properly and inevitably, was that she should serve the community, and not *vice versa*.

'I felt', she told me, 'that concern for the organization took precedence over concern for the individual.'

What I have been describing is not, of course, peculiar to our own day. It has always been inherent in the very existence of society. If the eclipse of the person behind the personage has taken on a new intensity in modern times, that is due to the technical development of our civilization, the concentration of the masses and the increasing mechanization of life. The peasant or the workman was once able to be himself in a way which is becoming impossible to most of our contemporaries.

The person is the original creation, the personage is the automatic routine. One effect of the increasing uniformity of life and of the crowding of people together in huge populations has been to mould vast numbers of them to a standard pattern. It is frightening sometimes to watch the crowd go by, catching the same bus every day šo as to arrive at the same time at the same office or factory, in order to perform some excessively specialized operation never requiring of them anything but the same robot-like movement.

They have become merely cogs in the machine of production, tools, functions. All that matters is what they do, not what they think or feel. In any case their thoughts and feelings are similarly moulded by propaganda, press, cinema and radio. They read the same newspaper each day, hear the same slogans, see the same advertisements.

All the blame, of course, does not rest with civilization. Look at the people who have worked hard for years to achieve a more comfortable standard of living. One might expect them to take the opportunity of indulging their fancy a little. But no: they prefer to go to the same old café, meet the same old companions, repeat the same conversations, spend their holidays in the same place. Automatic lives.

For their part those who aspire to live like real persons and not like automata find themselves caught in the toils of a mass society, against which originality rebels for a time, and then grows weary and is extinguished. The more people there are crowded together, the more does the herd-instinct develop. The massive undertaking in the long run turns its participants into automata. I have often had occasion to quote a remark made by Professor Siebeck: 'It is the calling that creates the person.' Modern Taylor-ized methods of work create only personages; they dehumanize men, depersonalize them. I need not labour the point: it has been stressed frequently by modern thinkers.

To this must be added the continued expansion of the power of the State, its control over the lives of individuals, and the abandonment to its anonymous intervention of more and more fields once reserved to private initiative. Regulations, forms and offices are multiplied, according to which human beings are

merely cases, documents or numbers. Clothed with their infinit-
esimal modicum of the impersonal authority of the State, civil
servants cannot, even with the best will in the world, take on
personal responsibilities outside their own limited competence.

Many industrial enterprises have reacted against this, and introduced psychology into the factory in an attempt to humanize it.
But, by an odd paradox, even this takes the form of standardized
psycho-technical tests, card indexes and statistics. Once again
it is the personage that is being measured, whose functions are
being explored, and which is being classified into categories.
Science knows nothing of the person.

Science develops techniques, increases the numbers of machines,
creates a whole artificial framework which deadens life. At the
last international conference on the medicine of the person one
of my colleagues, the medical superintendent of a big psychiatric
clinic, told us a story about his cowman. There is a large farm
attached to his clinic. The head cowman had given in his notice,
and the superintendent sent for him to ask him the reason for his
departure. 'They've bought electric machines for milking the
cows', he said, 'I haven't personal contact with my beasts any
more; I can't go on working under those conditions.'

This tendency towards mechanization is to be found in every
sphere of life, and it has the effect of dehumanizing civilization.
One of our sons is an architect, and I am acutely aware of the
problems that weigh on the minds of these young people in
search of a more human world. Less than a hundred years ago
the open space in front of the cathedral, the shopping streets in
the centre of the town and its picturesque little squares were
places where people could gather when the day's work was over.
They really met one another, as persons; they could take a stroll
together, talking peaceably, shake each other by the hand, forming groups that overflowed on the roadway.

Now the streets are invaded by motor-cars, dancing their
endless quadrille in time with the red, green and amber of the
traffic lights, and even mounting the pavement in order to find
a place to park. The public square was once the place where

one could feel the heart of the city beating—there one could meet one's friends, introduce them to others, and converse with them; it was the place where public opinion was freely born. Now one crosses it at speed, just managing to nod to one's acquaintances from a distance, through the car windows, when forced to stop in a traffic jam.

Nowadays in America you can even go to the cinema without getting out of your car. You drive into an immense car-park, and watch the film on a huge screen set up at one end, while all around the loud-speakers blare. The impersonality of the machine is invading our places of pleasure as well as our places of work.

A worker can spend years in a factory, shop or office, without meeting anyone who takes the slightest interest in him as a person, in his intimate concerns, in his difficulties or his secret aspirations. The daily routine, together with the prevailing atmosphere of our times, make it possible for him to associate with companions whom he really does not know, and who do not know him. He sees them only as they appear to be, and they see him only as a conventional personage.

Most of our contemporaries, dragooned and drowned in our mass society, caught in the vortex of speed, find themselves isolated in unbelievable spiritual solitude. They have no one with whom to share their secret burdens. Everyone is in a hurry, caught in the superficiality of a mechanized society.

It often happens that the doctor is the only one who in this modern world can offer an opportunity of personal fellowship. People expect him to understand them, for he has some experience of men and of life, and because his training inclines him towards particular cases rather than general ideas, because he is an observer and not a theorist. It is to him that people are most willing to show themselves as they are. The very act of undressing is a symbol of the casting off of the personage. This is well seen in Jules Romains' *Docteur Knock*, when a malicious villager comes to consult him just in order to annoy him. He is not at all so sure of himself when he is stark naked!

I have met many doctors either attached to factories or

practising in working-class areas who were fully aware of the great mission entrusted to them. Into the privacy of their consulting-rooms come one after another men who never have an opportunity anywhere else of talking intimately. The simplest anamnesis, if the doctor is attentive to the impulses of the soul, however slight, can open the door to confidences that have been too long held in check. Sickness, or perhaps the prospect of death, give rise to questions which the hectic rush of everyday life has kept in the background.

Such doctors have to engage in a relentless struggle against adverse conditions. Every new development in medicine has tended to make it more impersonal. There too there are more and more machines that remind one of the electric milker. It was well put by Professor Mach[1] while acting as chairman in a discussion on this subject at the 1952 International Geneva Conference: 'Where the sensitive and gentle hand of the doctor used to touch the patient's skin, now we have the cold and polished chrome steel surface of the electrical explorer.'

Science, with all the complicated problems its sets the mind of man, turns him away from those more basic problems that concern his life. The whole of their training tends to make doctors look rather at the mechanisms of the body and the mind than at the person. Science increases the doctor's prestige. My foreign visitor of whom I was speaking at the beginning of this chapter left with me some day-to-day notes he had written. They included a picturesque account of a recent visit to a highly-esteemed colleague of mine: all the majestic paraphernalia of white, the cold technical questions, the mysterious gestures! The description ended with the following note on the doctor: 'In short, he had donned the regalia of a Grand Master.'

Moreover, the need to specialize accords priority to the organ over the organism, turning medicine into a brilliant technique, automatized down to the last detail. Nothing, in my opinion, would be more serious than that the medicine of the person

[1] René-S. Mach, 'Médecine scientifique et respect de la personne', 1952 International Geneva Conference, in *Journal de Genève*, 12th September, 1952.

should come to be considered as a supplementary field of specialization reserved to a few rare doctors.

Finally, the legal status of medicine, and the development of social insurance everywhere, are rapidly transforming before our eyes the character of our profession. We are becoming like men working on a production belt, giving only the briefest of interviews to the patients who stream in endless succession through our surgeries.

Opening in Geneva the recent congress of the International Association for the Study of Bronchial Diseases, the President of the Swiss Confederation, Federal Councillor Rodolphe Rubattel, spoke on this subject. He spoke to the doctors there of the 'modern menace expressed in such words as speed, "automation", productivity, output, and others equally fearsome. . . .' He went on: 'It would be strange if the medicine we call "social", because it ought to benefit everybody without distinction of rank or wealth, were to finish up by divesting that benefit of its human substance, which consists in fellowship and sympathy. . . . Is not the doctor, in the long run, in peril of becoming in spite of himself a sort of super-controller, examining the visible signs of disease—analyses, diagrams, X-ray films—while failing adequately to associate with them those more personal pointers which the doctors of fifty years ago used to consider first?'

This is a pressing problem in the minds of many doctors today, and the solution to it is not easy to find. Obviously we cannot give up specialization, or refuse to avail ourselves of the resources of modern technique. Nor can there be any question of resisting a social trend which our very care for our fellows and their sufferings constrains us to welcome.

On consideration one sees that the solution does not lie so much in institutions as in the attitude of the doctor. However much of a specialist or a scientist he be, he can still be human if in his personal and spiritual life he retains the sense of the person. Then he will understand that the deepest and the universal suffering of men is that which each one carries in the secrecy of his heart, and which throughout his life compromises his health of body and mind. It is a suffering which is not revealed in a moment in an atmosphere of mechanization, nor can it be got rid of by means of hastily-scribbled prescriptions.

At medical conferences people have often protested to me that doctors have very little time at their disposal. Of course they cannot all give each patient as much time as a psychotherapist has to. But the experiences which had a decisive influence on the new direction my own career was to take, and which I spoke of in my first book, took place when I was a general practitioner. Humane medicine must not be confused with technical psychotherapy. The latter can be completely lacking in humanity, whereas general practice can be impregnated with it through and through. Often it is only a passing word which shows the patient that he is not merely a case in the eyes of his doctor, but a person.

We always find time for what we are interested in. There can be few vocations more interesting than that of seeking to understand the human person.

3

THIS CONTRADICTORY BEING

THERE ARE then, stubborn obstacles to be overcome in the search for the person. So far I have referred to those placed in our way by the outside world, and to the quite special way in which our modern age has increased their solidity. But the obstacles which we shall find within man himself are even more difficult to surmount. There is a man there in front of me, and I am listening attentively to what he is saying; but what is his real nature? He himself does not know. What he feels is that people habitually misjudge him. Society, his relations, his wife perhaps, summarily pronounce him mean or generous, active or lazy, brave or cowardly.

We have managed to establish that rare personal contact: we have had that profound experience of mutual recognition as human beings, in which both of us feel that it may lead us to the discovery of the person. Knowing a human being, however, calls for something more. The problem of his true nature is not resolved; I have but touched his person, behind the appearances of the personage. I have not penetrated it.

The more he tells me about himself, the more complex, even contradictory, does his person seem to be. We are all seething with contradictions; it is only with difficulty that we admit the fact to ourselves, and we take great care to hide it from others. It is perhaps as a form of escape from the vertigo which the full knowledge of this tangled complexity within us would cause, that we compose for ourselves a simpler personage. We do not have to explore the unconscious to find these contradictions, they are obvious whenever a man speaks to us frankly about himself.

Take the case of a certain politician of note. His great popularity has assured his re-election time and again. He is used to facing large crowds, and knows how to exert a powerful influence over them. In the privacy of the consulting-room he confesses to being fearfully timid. The other day he even refused an invitation to tea with a friend, so afraid was he that his hand would tremble as he held his cup, and betray the secret of his timidity.

Here, on the other hand, is a man in his forties who has not had the courage to come alone to his first consultation. His mother has brought him as if he were a ten-year-old, and is explaining the circumstances of his case. Meanwhile he sits in embarrassed silence, timidly perched on the edge of his chair, looking like the minor official he is. Now when contact is established, I shall discover that that man has the soul of an adventurer. He dreams of heroism and daring deeds, of distant voyages—though he has never left his mother's apron-strings. He reads avidly stories of exploration and detective novels, identifying himself with their most intrepid heroes.

You may say that this is mere dreaming, a secret life without real existence; that his true nature is this timorous appearance which he shows us. I do not think so. Much has been written— by myself as well as by other psychologists—about flight into dreams. But experience has prompted me to consider the subject further. Why is it that some people take refuge in dreams, while others are content with a humdrum existence? Is it not because there exists within them a call to which they have been unable to respond, and that this call in fact has something to tell us about their person? To write off their dreams as escapism, as smoke without fire, is to fail to understand the drama that is being played within them. There is no smoke without fire.

That man seems to me to be the victim of a small-minded and possessive mother. Here she is, still coming to speak for him; earlier in his life, when he was defenceless and entirely dependent upon her, she had prevented him from developing according to his own aspirations. She had been left a widow with this only child, and lived always in fear of losing her one remaining treasure. She had kept him constantly under her protection;

she refused him everything that contained the slightest element of risk; she chose his profession with only one thought in her mind: that of ensuring his security.

Of course the problem is even subtler than that. Let me try to explain one of its most difficult aspects. Education is not merely an external constraint. It insinuates itself into the very core of the child's being. There it sets up powerful reflexes. The result is that an inner conflict takes place between the spontaneous nature which cannot be destroyed, and these reflexes which prevent it from manifesting itself. This conflict paralyses spontaneous expression, cancelling out the two opposing forces.

In spite of all his mother's vigilance, her child sometimes escaped from her. He tells me of several incidents when he has been on the point of doing some daring act. It seems that at those moments it was audacity itself that he felt boiling up within him, a repressed potential of audacity. It frightened him, and set in motion the reflex that applied the brake, implanted in him by his mother. We apply the brake only when we feel a dangerous force. Thus the brake which clamps down on the whole of his life seems to me, in many respects, to be a sign of the authenticity of his daring impulses.

How many people have confessed to me that at certain moments in their lives they have been afraid of themselves, afraid of the forces at work within them, of their instincts, their desires, their feelings, and of the actions of which they felt themselves capable! It seems, then, that if these forces had in fact been less powerful, those people would have been more ready to let them show themselves. Excessive reserve may be the sign of excessive ardour.

You will note that I am having constantly to write "It seems. . .". That is a sign of the difficulty in which we find ourselves when we ask what is a man's true nature. The least one can say is that there is always some residue of doubt, that between the timid existence of this petty official and his secret life of adventure it is impossible to say with certainty which of them corresponds to his true nature.

48

To consider the first as his only real life because it is what we see, and to neglect the second, treating it as a hollow myth, would be a grave misunderstanding of the man. His bold life of fantasy is not less important to him because it is hidden; it means indeed much more to him than his poor daily routine. His heart is in his dreams; his quite automatic external appearance is rather something he puts up with. But it would be just as false to identify his person only with his adventurous self, and to see his timidity as no more than a garment, foreign to himself, which his up-bringing has forced him to don. Influences from without affect us only to the extent that they find us willing to accommodate them, just as an invader relies on a fifth column which conspires with him to deliver the place into his hands.

Another case will help us to define the problem more clearly. This again was a civil servant. He suffered acutely by reason of the discordance between the miserable façade of his life and the riches which he felt bubbling tumultuously within him. He was an artist who was never able to express himself—a real artist: I read some of the papers which he kept hidden in a drawer and never dared to set in order for publication. They witnessed to a rare talent. I came thus to know an aspect of his person which was hidden from the rest of the world.

Sartre seems to me to over-simplify the problem of man in flatly denying the existence of the confused inner life in which a piece of creative work is elaborated long before it is brought into manifest existence. 'The genius of Racine', he writes, 'is the series of his tragedies, outside of which there is nothing.'[1] This book that I am writing now has been in gestation in my mind for more than five years. If I had died a couple of months ago not a line of it would have seen the light of day. Nevertheless it would have been just as important for an understanding of me as a person, because the conception of a book is a far more decisive event than its actual writing down.

Before publishing my first book I showed my manuscript to

[1] Jean-Paul Sartre, *Existentialism and Humanism*, translated by Philip Mairet, Methuen and Co., London, 1948, p. 42.

some of my friends. I was so put off by the remarks they made, kindly meant though they were, that I did nothing with it for six months, incapable of writing a single sentence without at once judging it to be stupid. I nearly decided to give it up altogether.

You can imagine how exciting it is to find in lives that are apparently sterile the outline of many a book that never succeeds in being born because of external circumstances and internal doubts. It is impossible to say how much owes its origin to the inborn person, and how much is due to accident, in this passage from potential existence to 'existence' as Sartre understands it!

My friend the civil servant-artist realizes now that he has fashioned his apparent personage according to the picture his parents had of him. They always treated him as if he were incompetent, whereas they boasted about his brothers. The enemy within was the child's need for love, the potency of which the Freudians have brought out so clearly, and which drove him to become what his parents wanted him to be. The tragedy is that his parents' real motives in preferring their other children to him were of a quite different order, so that in acting as he did he was false to his own nature and still did not win the love he needed. The enemy within is also the false sense of guilt which is one of the unconscious factors pertaining to depth psychology.

But one does not have to analyse as deeply as that in order to see the quite incredible power of suggestion. If one thoughtlessly calls a child a liar, one makes him a liar, in spite of all his aspirations towards honesty. He is still at the age when the frontier between myth and reality is imprecise. People tell him fairy-stories; and if he too invents stories, he tells them as if they had really happened, and finds himself called a liar.

Call a child stupid, and you make him stupid, incapable of showing what he has it in him to do. A very pretty girl may always have been told by her mother that she is plain, either in order to preserve her from becoming conceited, or else from a subconscious motive which operates more often than one might imagine, namely, fear that she might outshine her mother. The girl comes to have so little confidence in her looks that if a man stares at her she mistakes his admiration for scorn.

The power of suggestion exercised by the labels we are given is considerable. This is particularly the case in childhood, but the same is true throughout our lives. A certain boy had a tendency towards effeminacy. When he was twelve his father died. His mother treated him like a girl to such an extent that she gave his father's razor to one of his cousins, with the remark: 'You'll never need it, anyway.' Unfortunately even we doctors are often guilty of saying thoughtlessly things which can have a dangerous suggestive effect on our patients; and the suggestion is all the more powerful because of the halo of scientific prestige with which we are invested. To tell a patient that he has a 'delicate liver' because he has vomited bile during a fit of bad-tempered annoyance, is to implant in his mind an idea of which he may never be able to rid himself, and which will be really harmful to his health.

The power of suggestion is readily seen if one considers the part it plays in politics, both national and international, where it is exploited by every party and every government. It seems that American statistics show that scarcely seven per cent of the population have independent minds. This means that it is possible to control the opinion of the vast majority of a nation. This seems so absurd to the people of other nations, who are themselves subjected to a contrary propaganda, that they suspect them all of insincerity, which is hardly credible. Each nation is more able to distinguish in others than in itself the motives of self-interest which govern public opinion, so that psychology usually throws light only on the behaviour of the people of other countries.

To the force of suggestion must be added that of habit, of which Pascal said that it is a second nature, and which we can see becoming part of our person. Only yesterday in the newspaper I came across a Spanish proverb: 'Habits begin like threads in a spider's web, but end up like ropes.' One of my patients is a young woman in whom the circumstances of her life have induced an attitude of constant resignation and abdication. For some months we have been working together, not without success, towards inner liberation for her. But she confesses to me that she still feels herself held back by the old habit. She is like a dog that has been chained so long to its kennel that by force of habit it keeps within the same limited radius even after it has been released.

Strange though it seems, people become used to suffering, even though they may rebel against it. Some experience an odd feeling of depression just at the point where difficulties from which they have suffered cruelly are resolved. It is as if they could no longer do without suffering, or as if they found themselves weak, because their strength depended on reaction against suffering. After a long period of rain we find difficulty in believing that we shall ever see blue sky again, however much we may long for it. The same applies to the meteorology of the soul.

Thus, as a result of the working of compensatory mechanisms, of suggestions and of habits, there develop within us contradictory tendencies, which gradually become more marked and permanent. The more divergent these tendencies are, the more effectively is the spontaneous stream of life dammed up. We are like those beginners in the art of ski-ing, who fall because they cannot keep their skis parallel, so that their legs are drawn too far apart. Every day I have in my consulting-room people who are torn like that between two contrary forces within themselves. The ones who are apparently the most timid are those who thirst most for fellowship. The one who seems most sociable is the one who is taking refuge in the ceaseless social round as an escape from intolerable inner loneliness. The man who seems to be completely sure of himself is really trying to bolster up his own lack of self-assurance by the way he behaves in front of others. The game he is playing will not escape the notice of his intuitive comrade, who may envy him and have a sense of inferiority beside him, and yet will say to me of him: 'You know, his self-assurance is just an act.'

I once lectured to an army audience on the subject of fear.

There was present on a courtesy visit a foreign officer who had been decorated for bravery during the war. He took part in the discussion, frankly acknowledging that he found it impossible to say whether it was courage or fear that had spurred him on. It seemed to me that he was giving the best proof of his courage in speaking to us as he did. But if, like him, we are sincere, we must recognize the profound uncertainty which surrounds the motives of our behaviour. Our motives are often quite different from what they seem. An intrepid Alpine climber once confessed to me that although everyone admired him, he knew himself to be a constant prey to fear. His love of taking risks was a way of giving that fear an object. Fear of a concrete danger is less unbearable than vague anxiety.

Everyone may think a certain individual vain, whereas the truth may be that he is completely unsure of himself and beset by feelings of inferiority. His ostentation is an attempt at compensation, which never quite succeeds. Others take pride in hiding their pride less naïvely. One man seems to be a self-assured go-getter, when in fact he is full of misgivings. Another is admired for his tireless devotion to his work, but confesses to me that all his feverish activity is really just a way of avoiding simpler but less agreeable tasks nearer home.

'At heart', he tells me, 'I believe I am lazy.'

One man always acts with impeccable correctness, but only with great difficulty does he admit to me what his behaviour is like in secret. Another always appears extremely serious-minded, but has childish habits which he carefully hides. A devoutly religious man lays bare to me the intolerable tragedy of his life: he is generally thought of as an example of serene piety, whereas in reality he is haunted constantly by sexual obsessions.

How many people there are who are one thing at home and something quite different outside! In their homes they have themselves waited on like Eastern potentates; outside they live lives of devotion to others. Authoritarian, tyrannical and argumentative at home; patient and conciliatory in the outside world. Silent and unapproachable at home; chatty and companionable outside. A pastor whose ministry is full of life and much appreciated, confesses himself incapable of praying alone with his wife. In all our hearts, faith is mixed with doubt, love with bitterness. I have dealt here with the contradictions of the human heart only from the psychological standpoint. I have not touched on the moral conflict, which St Paul describes in the Epistle to the Romans: 'For the good that I would I do not: but the evil which I would not, that I do' (Rom. 7.19).

It is extremely difficult for us to acknowledge this utterly illogical and contradictory character of our feelings. There comes to see me a young man who loves his father deeply, but who at the same time harbours a fierce hatred of him. We have to become very intimate before he can tell me what he feels. He is still afraid that I shall doubt his quite genuine love for his father if he confesses to the hostility he is capable of feeling towards him. One of Dr Maeder's patients protests his great admiration for his employer, who has done him grievous injury. The doctor must help him to confess to himself the contradictory feelings at work within him. 'Alongside admiration, and even love', he asks him, 'may there not also be room for hate in our hearts?'[1]

It is true that the most contrary feelings can live side by side in our hearts: hope and despair, joy and sorrow, anxiety and trust. I am reminded of a pious woman who had movingly laid bare to me the doubts that beset her. She had previously been to see her pastor, but he had cut the interview short, exclaiming: 'Doubts—a good Christian like you? Nonsense.'

It is possible for a mother to be very upset when her child is ill, and yet at the same time—perhaps without realizing it—derive a profound pleasure from looking after him. When he is well, he breaks away from her; but when he is ill he falls back into dependence upon her, and so gives her the instinctive satisfaction of playing the part of his protector. With the quick intuition that children have, he may feel that he is giving his mother pleasure,

[1] Alphonse Maeder, *Vers la guérison de l'âme*, Delachaux and Niestlé, Neuchâtel, 1946.

and this may hinder his recovery, and help to turn him into a sickly child.

It is the same with acceptance and rebellion. I have spoken elsewhere of how rebellion weakens the forces of life and healing within us. Acceptance of our diseases, our infirmities and the limitations imposed upon us by our nature and the circumstances of our existence, is the condition of that inner harmony which can play a decisive part in maintaining physical and moral health. Take for example acceptance of celibacy in women. A woman who had accepted it wholeheartedly, as the condition of a richer and more healthy life, even as a spiritual vocation, suddenly realizes that there is still rebellion against it in her heart, and that she must face it and overcome it anew every day. It is even possible that that woman's clearer self-vision will bring her to a more real self-denial than that attained by a woman who flatters herself that she has accepted her celibacy without any admixture of revolt.

In the same way a mother may suffer when she sees her child break away from her in order to take his place in the world, and at the same time be profoundly glad of it.

We are controlled by feelings, not by logic, though we fondly imagine that we are being guided by our reason. What happens in fact is that reason supplies the arguments with which to justify our behaviour. We appear to be logical, but are thoroughly illogical. That is one more contradiction.

In every encounter, from the simplest conversation between two friends, a ladies' sewing party, a gentlemen's club, a committee meeting, to the assemblies of scientific associations and great international political conferences, arguments are put forward in apparently objective and rational debate; but in reality each speaker is taking up and defending positions dictated by his instincts, his affectivity and his archetypal tendencies. Beneath the intellectual discussion we are moved all the time by fears, jealousies, childish admirations, unconscious projections.

A spiritual or intellectual experience is always accompanied by an emotional experience. We feel joy at being united with others

55

professing the same beliefs, people whom we love and who love us because we are engaged together in a common struggle. A person who has had this experience in a religious community or a political party, or through reading Karl Marx, St Thomas, Karl Barth or Rudolf Steiner, Freud, Bergson or Kierkegaard, will never tire of defending his master's system of thought, and will do it more passionately and uncompromisingly than the master himself. In such discussions how much real contact is there between the protagonists? How much real dialogue is there? It is rather a conflict of monologues, in which each is astonished that the logical arguments he is developing, which to him seem so compelling, do not at once convince the other.

Many a discussion would take quite a different course if we were to admit to each other the emotional and quite personal bases of our opinions: the bitterness against his father which turns a young man into an anarchist; the fear of losing his money which makes a rich man an adversary of communism; the jealousy which makes a committee-member oppose everything suggested by one of his colleagues; the desire for revenge which turns a young woman into a suffragette, because her father used to bully her mother, or which turns a man into an anti-feminist, because he is dominated by his wife.

I have just got back from a meeting of the steering committee of the *Rencontres internationales de médecine de la personne*. Since we are interested in the human person, we realize that the ideas and opinions of each of us are less objective than is commonly thought, and that they are closely connected with our own personal experiences. During the night I had had a dream which was clearly the manifestation of my unconscious reactions to our discussions of the previous day. In the morning I mentioned it to my friends. One of them, a psychoanalyst, began to question me about my associations of ideas, and made an analysis of my dream which threw a quite new light on the position I had taken up in the discussion. A surgeon, a Cartesian by up-bringing and unfamiliar with this type of inquiry, thought our interpretations rather far-fetched. But my own feeling was that we were touching a more solid reality than had been the case during our discussions of the previous day.

My psychoanalyst friend was particularly interested in one detail of the dream which still puzzled him: the bright red colour of a certain garment. At this point my wife joined us, not knowing anything of the matter we were discussing. He at once asked her:

'What do you think bright red symbolizes in a dream your husband has had?'

'That will be all the irritation he bottles up inside himself,' she replied.

'You think there is a lot of it?'

'Yes, I do! When something annoying happens I explode on the spot, but my husband remains quite calm; and when we talk about it afterwards he admits that he has been as irritated as I, but without showing it.'

We had spent the whole morning discussing the matter, but more had been done for our mutual understanding and for the unity of our group than if we had spent the time in intellectual argument.

On my way home I was thinking of the startling light that would be thrown on the discussions of any committee—even one composed of psychoanalysts—if one were to set about analysing the dreams of its members! Long-standing antagonisms would be explained at once, and would be much easier to resolve.

So far I have described human contradictions as we can all see them clearly displayed in our own hearts and in the acts of others. What if I were to hand over my pen to a specialist in the unconscious? What he discovers differs even more widely from the picture his patient has hitherto had of himself. Freud, firstly, has revealed the existence of a whole world of secret desires and all-powerful elementary drives which, disguised and unrecognized even by the individual himself, govern his behaviour, betraying themselves only in dreams and inadvertent actions. Adler has

shown the extent to which the personage is made up of compensations for an inferiority complex. Professor Jung has further
extended our knowledge of these unconscious mechanisms,
demonstrating the ancestral and collective elements in them, as
well as the spiritual factors which he calls archetypes.

One possible criticism of Freud is that having shown man to be
infinitely more complex than had been thought, he was then
guilty of over-simplification in the explanation of him which he
put forward, reducing the whole of his prodigious diversity to a
standardized schema.[1] The same complaint cannot be made in
the case of C. G. Jung. He himself has described[2] the almost
mystical emotion aroused in him by the realization of how
greatly men differ the one from the other, and what riches are
to be found in this diversity. He had of course already observed
it, but one day he came to a deeper understanding of it, an
understanding which has preserved him from arbitrary general-
izations.

In Jung we find our problem of the person becoming im-
measurably more complex. The psychology of the unconscious
gives us a picture of man made up entirely of mutually opposite
tendencies: intellect and feeling, intuition and the sense of reality,
'animus', the logical masculine principle, and 'anima', the
affective feminine principle. 'As a general rule', he writes, 'the
tenor of the unconscious forms a contrast with the conscious
state.'

We have daily confirmation of this fact. There is, firstly, the
opposition described by Freud between the amoral drives of
instinct and the conscious moral code inculcated by education
and the dictates of society. One of my patients, a woman, once
said to me in all sincerity: 'My inmost soul is quite pure.' Another
remarked once: 'Until now I had thought myself to be without
any sexual instinct.' And only the other day a woman obsessed

[1] See Georges Gusdorf, *La découverte de soi*, Presses universitaires de France,
Paris, 1953.

[2] C. G. Jung, *L'homme à la découverte de son âme*, Editions du Mont-Blanc,
Geneva, 1944.

by scruples of quite a different kind said: 'Sex has never been one of my problems.' I sent her of course to a Freudian colleague of mine, in whose hands patients like her recognize themselves to be quite different from what they believed. It is the Freudians also who have shown us how many infantile attitudes and reactions persist into what we fondly call adulthood. A strong, aloof, austere woman discovers the repressed longing to be coddled which still lies hidden deep within her. An impotent man perceives that his infirmity is but a mask to hide a temperament so potent that he is afraid of it; and then that the indifference he now feels with regard to women is a second mask, hiding the first.

But there are many contradictions in man as revealed to us by Jung. There is the intellectual, for instance, so exclusively intellectual apparently that even religion is for him no more than a series of reasoned propositions; for whom a game or a sport becomes a science, a calculation, a methodical study devoid of any fantasy or pleasure. And yet without knowing it he is a sentimentalist: he even hesitates to go to the theatre because he is ashamed of the tears that come all too readily to his eyes.

There is the positivist who thinks himself free of all metaphysical preoccupations, and yet confesses that he is beset by religious longings that have never come to the surface of his consciousness.

There is the man suffering from depression who for years has gone from doctor to doctor, convinced that he has a cancerous growth which they all fail to recognize, and which threatens him with imminent death. His heart is full of such anxiety and despair that he can find no words strong enough to express it. Nevertheless, there must be some hope lingering within him, for he often dreams that he is making difficult journeys in a carriage or car, in which the vehicle gets stuck in deep ruts, encounters numerous obstacles, breaks down, or toils up a precipitous slope. He always manages to extricate himself, to pass round the obstacles, to get his vehicle going again and to reach the top of the hill. He feels exhausted, thinks he has no strength left, and expects only help from outside in the form of medicine and surgery. One of his dreams is that he goes to make a purchase in a shop, fails to find the article he requires, and remembers just at that moment that he has what he needs at home all the time.

There is the idealist who has 'repressed his shadow', that is to say, closed his eyes to everything in himself which he finds displeasing, and who tells me with an openness which is obviously sincere: 'I have no sin'. I am sure that his wife would not agree with him; but he has no inkling of the suffering he inflicts on her as he devotes himself to noble crusades in the name of justice. There is the repression of the moral conscience so well described by Professor Baruk,[1] in which he sees the hidden source of aggressiveness (unlike the Freudians, who consider aggressiveness to be a primitive impulse).

The reader will see that the tremendous advance that has taken place in our psychological knowledge in the course of the last half-century has created more problems than it has solved. Man is seen to be ever more complicated, contradictory and elusive. What is the reality, the authentic person behind all its camouflage? I have seen sick people and healthy ones too, whose minds reel when presented with this psychoanalytical perspective. All their preconceived ideas about themselves crumble away, and they wonder if there are such things as good and evil, if truth has any meaning, or if they can be certain about anything.

Psychological analysis, of course, does nothing to remove the contradictions of the human heart. Psychoanalysts would be the first to admit this. Their methods are only a way of treating inhibitions and serious psychical disturbances, a means of giving back to their patients some capacity for happiness, for normal activity and social life. But after months and even years of analytic treatment they remain, like you and me, full of complexes, inner conflicts and ambivalent tendencies. The history of this word ambivalence is an eloquent testimony to the fact that the more

[1] H. Baruk, *Psychiatrie morale expérimentale*, Presses universitaires de France, Paris, 1945.

we study man, the more do we find him divided between contrary feelings and aspirations.

What Professor Jung calls 'integration',[1] is not at all a simplification of the mind. On the contrary, it is a progressive realization of one's secret propensities, and a lucid and courageous acceptance of the totality of one's being, with all its complications and contradictions. The work that has been done in this field is tremendously interesting as well as being of practical value. But the problem of the person is still unsolved.

In fact, a very serious question is raised. Analysis shows that the motions of the unconscious are quite different from those of our conscious life. Can we then say that these unconscious impulsions are our true nature, and that our conscious life is but an alien garment, a personage, which we have donned under the influence of education or of psychial mechanisms of camouflage? The psychoanalysts, to judge from their writings, seem to incline towards this view. I myself wrote just now of an apparently vain man that he was in reality a prey to doubts about himself and to feelings of inferiority.

The expression 'in reality' comes readily to the pen, so striking is the discovery of a secret reality which explains the external reality. But it lends itself to misunderstanding in that it suggests that the unconscious life alone is real. Classical psychology, confining itself to a formal list of 'faculties of the mind', knew nothing of the unconscious factors revealed by depth psychology. The latter, in its turn, is now in danger of underestimating the importance of the conscious life of the mind. Take, for instance, the case of a man whose life has been nothing but a series of failures. Classical psychology considered him as being deficient in will-power. Depth psychology offers a much more penetrating interpretation.

Practical experience, however, has shown me that the discovery of the unconscious mechanisms which underlie his failures is not in itself sufficient to cure him. What is needed in a real sense is re-education, which I do not believe any psychotherapist can

[1] *Op. cit.*

accomplish without calling, either explicitly or implicitly, upon the conscious energies of his patient. Professor Baudouin has shown the preponderant role accorded, in psychism, to 'the force of the idea and the forces of the heart', He also says, however, that 'the truly voluntary act retains its full value'.[1]

Once more, then, we are put on our guard against oversimplification in our view of man, through underestimating either his unconscious or his conscious life. We must accept him in his entirety, with all his contradictions, with all the forces both conscious and unconscious at work within him. All the forces and mechanisms studied by science belong to the personage. The person is not to be reduced any more to the mechanisms of the unconscious than to the workings of the conscious faculties. It remains hidden from objective observation.

The characteristic that inclines many modern psychologists to attach more importance to the unconscious factors and to identify them to a greater or less degree with the true person, is their immutability. 'The unconscious is never transformed', writes Dr Jung.[2] If someone asks for my photograph, would I give him a radiograph of my skull, on the grounds that it alone does not change, whereas the features of my face alter from moment to moment? In spite of its inconsistency—even because of it—my physiognomy in its constant fluidity expresses what is personal to me far better than does my bony structure, in which I am more like all other men.

Furthermore, it is by no means certain that what we discover in the unconscious is any more objective. A young man reports to me a 'big' dream, a magnificent dream, a dream 'à la Jung', which delights me as it would surely delight Professor Jung himself. But this young man confesses that the day before he had actually been reading one of Jung's books, and had longed to have a dream himself as fine as those he had read about. To what extent has his unconscious fabricated what he wanted to be

1 Charles Baudouin, *La force en nous*, Delachaux and Niestlé, Neuchâtel, 1950.
2 *Op. cit.*

able to bring to me? This is a case like that of the children I mentioned earlier, who form their personage in accordance with their parents' wishes, in order to please them.

It is a well-known fact that when a course of psychoanalysis is going well, the patient begins to have more dreams, and that the dreams stop if he is in conflict with his psychoanalyst. If I am especially interested in the Freudian mechanisms of a patient's behaviour, he produces for me abundant signs of his sexual repressions and infantile regressions. If I show myself more interested in a Jungian interpretation of the same patient's case, he will produce the appropriate data.

Thus we come back to what I showed at the beginning of this book, that the person of the observer himself contributes as much as that of the individual observed to the result of the observation. This has far-reaching implications. Not even therapeutic efficacy can be taken as a safe criterion; for it is clear that if the patient pleases his doctor by bringing him material which confirms his theories, he is at the same time creating conditions favourable to transference, which is a major factor in effecting a cure. In relation to his doctor he is in the situation of the child who develops because he feels that his father is pleased with him and proud of him.

PART TWO

LIFE

4

UTOPIA

AFTER ALL we have said so far, the reader will not be surprised at a remark made by Professor Gusdorf in a recent book,[1] to the effect that introspection has failed completely as a means of discovering the person. I found his book particularly interesting, since with the erudition and clarity of the trained philosopher it gave the explanation of the things which practical experience in the consulting-room was daily bringing to my notice.

Professor Gusdorf first reminds us that the Ancients did not concern themselves with the individual, but only with formulating a conceptual type of man. Even when Socrates undertook in his dialogues to 'reveal to those to whom he was speaking unsuspected conflicts within themselves', his aim was not to apprehend them in their 'particularity', but rather to bring out a preconceived 'normative idea' of man. 'In his *Cratylus* we see him glimpsing the abyss of indefinite analysis', which he was careful to avoid.

With Montaigne, on the other hand, there appears a new attitude, that of introspection. In order to discover himself as he is, man sets out to examine himself without any preconceived ideas or doctrinaire prejudices: 'I do not teach, I tell', writes Montaigne in his *Essays*, adding: 'Only you yourself know whether you are cowardly and cruel, or loyal and devout; others do not see you, they make but uncertain conjectures about you; they see not so much your nature as your art.'

This new attitude reached its fullest expression in the work of Jean-Jacques Rousseau, who, in the introduction to his *Confessions*, boasted that for the first time in history he was giving 'a portrait

[1] *Op. cit.*

67

in every way true to nature'.[1] From then on sincerity was considered as being the necessary and sufficient condition of the
discovery of self. 'Sincerity towards oneself is, as everyone knows,
the virtue of our generation,' said François Mauriac.[2]

The attempt to express oneself in a personal diary, so much in
vogue and so characteristic of modern times, proceeds from this
attitude. My compatriot H. F. Amiel devoted a lifetime of
meticulous care to it.[3] Anyone who tries as honestly as he to
arrive by this method at real self-knowledge will recognize—
as he does—that the effort is doomed to failure. The essential
always escapes one's grasp: 'What a false idea of myself [this
journal] would give, if anyone happened to read it. . . . There is
my work, this book which is coming to birth within my mind
at every hour of the day, there is my reading, there are thoughts
of which I do not speak at all,' writes Julien Green; and later:
'Is it really possible to keep a journal which gives an approxi-
mately accurate impression of its author? I am beginning to doubt
it.'[4]

Introspection does not throw any sure light on oneself: 'I am
thirty-six, and I do not know yet whether I am miserly or
prodigal, sober or gluttonous.'[5] These words from the pen of
André Gide are a tragic reply to Montaigne's remark which I
quoted just now. Moreover, introspection actually alters the
person. Paul Claudel writes: 'Merely by looking at ourselves we
falsify ourselves.'[6] Self-examination is an exhausting undertaking.
The mind becomes so engrossed in it that it loses its normal
capacity for relationship with the world and with God. Locked

[1] Jean-Jacques Rousseau, *Confessions*, translated by J. M. Cohen, Penguin
Books, London, 1953.
[2] Quoted in Thibaudet, *Réflexions sur la littérature*, N. R. F., Paris, 1940.
[3] H. F. Amiel, *The private Journal of Henri Frédéric Amiel*, translated by
Van Wyck Brooks and Charles Van Wyck Brooks, MacMillan & Co., New
York, 1935.
[4] Julien Green, *Personal Record, 1928-1939*, translated by Jocelyn Godefroi,
Hamish Hamilton, London, p. 52 and p. 340.
[5] A. Gide, *Journal*, N. R. F., Paris.
[6] Paul Claudel, 'Déclarations à Frédéric Lefèvre', in *Nouvelles littéraires*,
Paris, 18th April, 1925.

in a narrow round of endless and sterile self-analysis, the person becomes shrunk and deformed, while false problems multiply *ad infinitum*.

That shrewd judge of human nature, Saint Francis de Sales, had already written: 'It is not possible that the Spirit of God should dwell in a mind that wishes to know too much of what is happening within itself. . . . You are afraid of being afraid, then you are afraid of being afraid of being afraid. Some vexation vexes you, and then you are vexed at being vexed by that vexation. In the same way I have often seen people who, having lost their tempers, are afterwards angry at having been angry. All this is like the circles made when a stone is cast into the water—first a little circle forms, and that in its turn makes a bigger one, and that one makes yet another.'[1]

We can understand now André Gide's bitter cry: 'What has happened to me? I have killed my youth, its innocent freshness. . . .' Elsewhere he writes: 'The desire to write the pages of this journal well, destroys any merit they might have, even that of sincerity.'[2] Amiel, too, always in quest of the truth about his own person, comes at last to the point of saying: 'He [the thinker] depersonalizes himself.'[3] And Nietzsche: 'Everyone is furthest from himself.'[4] Professor Gusdorf concludes: 'It seems that sincerity is an unattainable ideal.'[5]

Adolescence is the age for the writing of diaries. Those who keep it up all their lives, so far from attaining the desired maturity, remain perpetually adolescent. Now, Professor Jung has shown us that adolescence is the age of idealism, of the 'repression of the shadow', the age of the completest misunderstanding of oneself.

[1] Quoted by T. Feugère, *Le Mouvement religieux dans la littérature du XVIIᵉ siècle*, Boivin, 1938. Cf. Allan Ross's English translation of Saint Francis de Sales' *Introduction to the Devout Life*, Burnes Oates and Washbourne, London, 1943, pp. 137-8.

[2] *Op. cit.*

[3] *Op. cit.*, p. 620.

[4] Friedrich Nietzsche, *The Joyful Wisdom*, translated by Thomas Common, T. N. Foulis, Edinburgh, 1910, p. 259.

[5] *Op. cit.*

These perpetual adolescents are in fact those who have not succeeded in 'integrating' their persons, in attaining a state of awareness of the totality of themselves.

Many of those who come to see me entrust their diaries to me. I always expend a considerable amount of time and care over the reading of them, for I feel that the confidence thus shown in me warrants my respect. I must say that the effort has never seemed to me to be wasted: it is always interesting to have new light thrown on a person's life, even if it means wading through long rambling stories to find the hastily scribbled note which is often the most illuminating thing in the diary. This last remark shows that the value of a diary lies in its often contradictory elements rather than in any general picture it may present. It is a series of sketches of varying states of mind that are often difficult to reconcile with each other, rather than a coherent account of the person.

Man remains a mystery to himself, and to attempt to elucidate that mystery by delving into one's mind is merely to increase its perplexing obscurity. I have received a long letter from a woman, a stranger to me, in which she recounts her whole life-story. She is herself astonished by her own inexplicable conduct in many different circumstances, and concludes: 'When I was a girl I wanted to join the Little Sisters of the Poor—but I still do not know whether I was cut out for that, or just to be a trollop!'

We are, then, pursuing a chimera in attempting to grasp the essence of our person, completely divested of all adornments and disguises with which life has clothed it. One thing that would have to be got rid of would be memory, which is a fundamental property of life; that would mean getting rid of life itself. Even if we could succeed in doing that, we should not be laying hold on the living person, but on a mummy, a skeleton-like caricature of the person. All that we have lived through and felt in the past is inscribed in us, and helps to make us what we are today. However artificial and contradictory each of our feelings and acts have been, they are still active and ineffaceable elements of ourselves.

I do not say that this delving into ourselves is entirely valueless; it opens up a rich field for discovery; the trouble is that it is too rich. Every time we are sincere about it we see that some attitude which we thought we had taken up spontaneously is in fact the result of mechanisms which, because they are more deep-seated, we take to be more authentically personal. An experience of that sort is always moving and humbling, as well as fruitful. We have the impression, or rather the overwhelming conviction, that we are seeing ourselves to be quite different from what we supposed. But it is an exploration which can go on for ever. If our sincerity is exacting, we soon see that we have doffed one garment only to find another beneath it.

In fact, what in the blinding light of the discovery we have taken to be our true person, is still only an aspect of it—a real one, certainly, but incomplete. On analysis it proves once more to be determined by deeper mechanisms. And so we could go on, until we reached the unconscious forces which are no longer personal at all: the impulsions of instinct, noted by Freud, which we possess in common with the animals, or the ancestral archetypes of the collective unconscious, described by Jung, which we have in common with all other human beings. We should then be in the presence only of completely impersonal forces of nature.

Thus, the result of our quest is that the person, through having its successive envelopes peeled off one by one, vanishes in our hands. One can understand, then, Shri Ramakrishna's remark: 'Think well, and you will see that there is nothing you can call "I". As you peel an onion, there is always another layer, but you never reach the kernel. So when you analyse the ego, it disappears completely.'[1]

Are we then to conclude that our most superficial, most accidental and artificial characteristics are the most personal thing about us? We intuitively rebel against such an idea. And yet practical observation seems constantly to give the lie to that intuition. Take, for example, the case of a young woman with

[1] Shri Ramakrishna, *Message actuel de l'Inde*. Les Cahiers du Sud, Paris.

whom I have had a number of very candid conversations. She is an orphan, crushed as it were by life, held back constantly by ill-health. We have been able to see together how far suggestions by those about her, her own habits, painful experiences both long past and recent, unconscious factors and the false reactions which hide them have gone to make up the personage she appears to be.

But what is she in reality? We may think we can guess—but she never succeeds in showing us. Can we call a thing which never manifests itself a reality? Can we believe it to be more real than these appearances that weigh on her like burdens she cannot shed? Are we not deluding ourselves in believing we discern a being instinct with abundant life behind this death-mask? She told me one day that she felt herself caught in an impasse: she had come to realize the impossibility of disregarding the influences, external and internal, which distort our view of ourselves. We parted in an atmosphere of deep sadness.

The next day something quite unexpected happened: she underwent a spiritual experience. I had unwittingly helped to bring it about by a remark which I did not even remember having made, when she spoke to me about it later. I know what it is to be an orphan myself, and I live my earthly life in the hope of finding my parents again in the heavenly resurrection. I had spoken to her of this hope, but only incidentally, without any calculated intention. Something happened inside her which suddenly changed her whole outlook. She expressed it to me thus: 'Until that moment I had always felt myself the orphan of a corpse. But all at once I realized that I was the orphan of someone resurrected and living.'

I believe that our honest search to find the truth about her real person helped to prepare the way for this spiritual experience. A breath of new life broke in upon her soul. But this was an event of quite a new kind, not an inventory of her person, but its awakening; not an intellectual analysis, but a living manifestation. Such an event does not remove our inability to separate the person from the personage, but it does something more.

It seems that we must resign ourselves to this indissoluble

connection between the person and its personage—or rather, between the person and its personages. For we are not only one personage throughout our lives; we are innumerable personages. At each new encounter we show ourselves different; with one friend we are the serious thinker; with another, the wag; we change our demeanour to suit each new situation. We are even many personages at once.

There is in me the troubled and anxious man, full of doubts about himself and about everything else, who himself knows all the anxieties and all the failures that my patients come to confess to me. There is in me the steadfast believer, who has had solid experience of God's grace, and who witnesses to it with conviction. In me there is one who wishes to see himself and show himself, clearly, as he is; and there is one who wishes to parade even this honest desire. There is in me the doctor who believes passionately in his medicine, and eagerly runs to help his fellow-men; there is in me the egoist and sceptic, who would like to run away and hide in a solitary cabin.

The person, whatever it be, can only be manifested by expressing itself; and expression means a personage. I write these lines in French, in a language which I learnt at school and in the street, which I have received from Society, which is a complete social convention. I can scarcely think without enclosing my thought in words which are not personal to me, but common to all those who speak the same language. All the authors I have read have imparted to those words the associations which they have for me. Even in my dreams, I utter and hear sentences which, to be understood, must obey grammatical rules which the French Academy itself is powerless to alter.[1]

It is true that the language of dreams is pictures rather than words. But the psychoanalysts have shown that that language is not personal either. No matter to what nation or civilization the dreamer belongs, whether he be cultured or not, his dreams show the same Freudian symbols and the same Jungian archetypes.

[1] See Georges Gusdorf, *La parole*, Presses universitaires de France, Paris, 1953.

We find them in the fairy-tales, legends and folklore of every country.[1] Each of us bears inscribed in his soul all the eternal verities of mythology, all the universal images of poetry. These traditional forms are not indeed personages, but personage-types, not individual personages. This is the very basis of poetry. The emotion which poetry awakens in us is the encounter between the image evoked by the poet and the same image which sleeps within ourselves, ready to be awakened by the contact.

The whole of art, however personal it seems or tries to seem, is essentially communion, a bond between persons, a supra-personal and inter-personal reality. Cartesians always affirm the primacy of reason, the language of which they hold to be universal. But the language of images, of poetry and art is universal also. There is no drama without convention, no photography even, without social convention. My dog does not recognize his photograph—to him it is only a blackened piece of paper.

The case of the ultra-modern artist is no different; his genius goes more or less against the conventions of his day, and therefore wins only tardy recognition; but he is helping to form new conventions. He succeeds in this because his genius is less original than it seemed, and awakens common echoes in the human heart. If he could be absolutely personal, he would remain absolutely alone, and he would not be an artist. In music our generation has witnessed an unparalleled revolution. I have seen a large number of young people whose parents disapproved violently of their addiction to jazz, even describing them as degenerate. I belong to the parents' generation, and it was only after these young people had confided intimately to me what the new music meant to them that I found that it had the power to awaken in me also secret echoes whose presence I had not suspected.

I should like to make one remark in this connection: a thing that strikes me about a great many people is the way they declare themselves to be 'shocked' every time they meet some unaccustomed form of expression. They at once take up a hostile

[1] See Leïa, *Le symbolisme des contes de fées*, Editions du Mont-Blanc, Geneva, 1943.

attitude towards it, as if their own personage must be defended against this alien one. This tends to make them narrow, to imprison them within their traditional forms. If, on the other hand, one takes pleasure in discovering and understanding what was hitherto unknown, every new encounter becomes an occasion for growth and self-liberation.

So, if we tried to cast off all our social apparel, we should tend to become individuals and not persons. The notion of the person is bound up with the human community, a spiritual solidarity, a common patrimony, and therefore to a certain conventional form of expression which partakes of the nature of the personage. When we meet someone, we seek personal contact, but one of its conditions is a certain mutual intelligibility in our modes of expression which is of the order of the personage.

If I speak neither the language of reason nor that of poetry, I speak by my glance, my smile, my silence, my gestures and the demeanour I adopt. Consider this, and you will see that there must always enter into these things some measure of convention, which varies with the country and the period. Even the lover in his transports uses such hackneyed expressions, such well-worn gestures, that the lady he loves, were she to remain cool and clear-headed, must think him a very third-rate actor. She would soon detect re-hashed Lamartine or Stendhal, or Hollywood, and would perhaps mistake his genuinely spontaneous utterances for conscious imitation.

Almost the only emotional manifestations which can escape the charge of artificiality are those which are really physiological, like tears. And even then—I have known many families where no one ever wept, even on occasions such as bereavement; and more than one man or woman has told me that they hesitated to come to see me for fear of weeping as they recounted their troubles. And yet it is with the sudden furtive tear or the almost imperceptible smile that one senses the presence of the person hidden behind the habitual personage. These people want to discover themselves, and they are at the same time afraid of uncovering themselves. I am told that in the Far East, where death is certainly not viewed in the same emotional light as with us, they make a great noise when a death has taken place, in order to drive evil spirits away; they use professional weepers, who have themselves no cause for sorrow, while those who are in sorrow do not weep. No civilization has paid such attention to the principle of saving face.

It would seem that nudists—at any rate some of them—sincerely pursue the paradisiac and utopian dream of a complete divesting of the formal personage in the hope of creating a more genuine human community. To reveal oneself in all simplicity, just as one is, without even hiding what elementary modesty prompts one to conceal, is meant to be the symbol of a renunciation of all hypocrisy. Often our patients tell us of dreams in which they have seen themselves naked, and this always represents an inner longing to cast away their mask. I speak of nudism only with caution, for it deserves a thorough study. But I have felt that in fact this 'idealist' dream of an innocent society is the mark of a psychological disturbance. This would explain the attraction exercised by nudism on people who suffer from unconscious repressions.

On this subject there is a passage in the Bible which is very much to the point. After the Fall, Adam and Eve provided themselves with a covering by sewing fig-leaves together to make aprons (Gen. 3.7). But God himself soon came and perfected their rudimentary art, making them clothing of skins (Gen. 3.21). For he knew that thenceforth, in our human condition, and until the redemption of the world should be accomplished, we might no more be completely naked persons. Instead of taking man's clothing away from him, God provides him with a finer garment. Later, St Paul, after exhorting us to put off the old man, invites us to put on the new man, born of the Spirit (Col. 3.9-10). He speaks also of putting on the breastplate of righteousness, the helmet of salvation, and the girdle of truth (Eph. 6.14-16).

So, with its characteristic realism, the biblical revelation turns us from the utopian dream of a life exempt from all appearance and all protection. For the efforts we were vainly making to isolate our person completely from our personage it substitutes a quite different idea: that of accepting the clothing which God himself gives us, of choosing our personage—the personage God wills us to have.

The Bible does not despise *décor*. It sees the whole of nature as the splendid setting which God has provided for our lives. It sings of the beauty of woman, the splendours of Solomon's Temple, the poetry of the countryside, the glory of flowers. It speaks of sumptuous garments, ornaments of gold and silver, music and dancing, ritual and pious customs. It requires us to do well everything that we do, to pay attention, that is, to its form, for God is not a God of disorder (I Cor. 14.33). 'He that ruleth, [let him do it] with diligence' (Rom. 12.8).

The Bohemian who affects to despise conventions is not on that account without a personage. He has simply chosen one which he considers to be more original, and takes as much pride in it as the dandy in his sartorial elegance.

I once lectured abroad on this subject. While I was sitting in a restaurant going over my notes, I watched the waiters setting the tables. They saw that the table-cloths were hanging evenly over the edges of the tables; they laid the places with perfect symmetry; they folded the serviettes with artistic care. I observed the curtains carefully chosen by the proprietor, the harmony of the colour-scheme, the attention that had been given to the smallest detail in order to please the customers even without their noticing it. Everything betokened a professional sense of responsibility and a love of their work which was of undoubted value.

I myself, as I write this book, take care to arrange the parts and chapters harmoniously, and feel dissatisfied if one of them gets too long and so threatens to throw the whole book out of balance. I feel it would be disrespectful to my readers. This is a concern of an architectural nature, which aptly expresses a genuine bent in my person. Thus every function in the world entails its own requirements, and calls for the observance of certain forms, and to conform to them is not mere play-acting.

Recently I had an important discussion with some friends who are surgeons.

'I have been thinking for years about the questions you raise', one of them said to me, 'but in surgery it isn't easy. I recognize that the patient needs to have personal contact with his doctor; but the best surgeons are not those who talk to their patients most. In the town where I practice the acknowledged master is a man of very few words. He spends a long time examining the patient in complete silence, and then suddenly pronounces his verdict: "I operate on you tomorrow morning." His hesitations, his very real human sympathy, he keeps hidden. What the patient sees is a sober personage acting decisively, and this inspires in him such complete confidence that he goes to the operating-table without the slightest apprehension.'

That surgeon's remarks reminded me of the following words, written by a doctor, André Sarradon: 'We must put on this personage in the measure that our patients expect it of us.'[1]

The courts of kings are governed by protocol, and however they may wish to avoid some too pompous solemnity, they must submit to it in order to honour the people whom they represent. The supreme virtue of kings is precisely this renunciation of personal caprice, in order to act the role required of them by their vocation, identifying themselves with the personage they are compelled to be, and never forgetting that they are kings.

I had occasion recently to visit a big health resort in the Alps. It was the day after St Catherine's Day. On that day a masked fancy-dress ball is held in each sanatorium. The medical superintendents told me that they never miss attending these functions, because there they can glean information about the persons of their patients which they miss in the routine of day-to-day life. Why does this woman disguise herself as a man, or that one choose to dress up as the traditional witless country-girl or the wicked fairy of the folk-tales? It is no mere accident!

And then, wearing masks, the patients behave differently from

[1] André Sarradon, *La personne du médecin*, unpublished.

usual. They reveal facets of their person that are normally con-
cealed. So, by a curious paradox, the costume and mask, instead
of hiding the person, actually display it with greater truth. Is not
this what Buffon meant by his famous remark: 'The style is
the man himself?' I am always a little put out when instead of
discussing the facts and ideas in my books, people compliment me
on my style! 'You have the knack of expressing what I have
thought for a long time without being able to put it into words.'

We always tend to think of form and substance as opposites,
and we would rather the substance of our work were appreciated
than the form. But this differentiation is naïve and pretentious:
the form is what is seen, and we always like to flatter ourselves
(with regard to ourselves as well as to others) that what is not seen
is more valuable than what is seen. 'The exterior is the signature
of the interior,' wrote Jacob Boehme.

The same is true of the whole of life. The personage we put on
is not as artificial as we think. It expresses our real person all
the more faithfully because we are less on our guard with respect
to it. When one of my patients is talking to me, and trying most
carefully to express his real self, his mechanical gestures and his
unpremeditated attitudes also speak to me, and furnish information about him which is quite as valuable as what he says.

The occupation I have chosen, the arrangement of my study,
where I go for my holidays, the whole setting of my life, all the
external appearance which makes up my personage, is inseparable
from my person, because it is the expression of it. A woman
buying a dress is well aware of this; and so is the shop-assistant
who tells her: 'This one suits you perfectly! And it's a Paris
model; you won't see another one like it. It's *your* dress. It's
quite personal.' We see here the subtle interplay of social and
personal factors: nothing is more conventional than the fashion
which imposes on all women certain forms of expression, and a
certain style on a whole period. The woman who does not submit to it is guilty of lack of taste; but if she follows it too slavishly,
wearing a mass-produced dress which is to be seen everywhere,
she shows lack of personality.

Our personage moulds our person. The external role we play transforms us constantly, exerting its influence even on the deepest and most intimate recesses of the person. Of course, the habit does not make the monk—the proverb is an indication of the subtlety of the problem—putting on a dress will not turn us into a saint. But neither is it without good reason that a priest wears a cassock, a judge his robe, or the soldier his uniform. (Do you remember those August days of 1939, when the German radio played military marches from morning to night?) Napoleon knew what he was talking about when he wrote: 'One becomes the man of one's uniform.'[1]

Propaganda comes to us from without, but it penetrates our deepest selves. The demeanour we adopt, every gesture we make, similarly play their part in fashioning us inwardly. It is actually possible to modify the character by a systematic reform of hand-writing. Even our physical constitution is influenced by the personage we put on. Caricaturists know this well; I always remember a miser who looked as if he had been drawn by a particularly mordant caricaturist, with his nose and chin almost meeting, and his nails curved in a complete semicircle.

Thus our physical, psychical, and even our spiritual life bear the imprint of our personage. I have already told the story of the friend who used to ask everybody what he must do to find faith. It was a sort of challenge, for he used to add: 'You say that it is a matter of grace, so there is nothing I can do about it.'

One day he was given the answer: 'Begin by living as if you had faith, and you will see.'

Thinking it over, my friend realized that the challenge had been thrown back at him: he knew well enough what he had to change in his life. When he had done it, he did find faith.

The ground of our problem has shifted. We turn our backs on the utopian dream of living nakedly, of shedding the personage from the person. We recognize that they are inseparable. But why is it, then, that we are obsessed with the idea of distin-guishing and separating them? Whence comes the uneasy feeling

[1] Quoted in *Petit écho de la mode*, Paris, 11th July, 1954.

which we all experience when we see ourselves and others acting a part?

One of my patients once said to me: 'There is something in me which protests—when I am at the theatre, for example, watching a magnificent production, I seem to hear a voice inside me telling me the whole thing is grotesque.' She went on: 'What irks me is the thought that it has been arranged in order to be magnificent.' It is not the mask, the personage in itself, but its artificial and deceptive character, which gives us the uneasy feeling I was speaking of. It happens as soon as we perceive a discord between the person and the personage.

It is not, then, a case of casting off the personage, but of bringing it into harmony with the person. It is a case of being in accord with oneself. Pindar put it magnificently: 'Become what you are.' We must turn about, and proceed in an entirely new direction. Instead of turning our backs on the outside world and concentrating on our own inner life, where the true nature of the person always eludes us, we must look outwards, towards the world, towards our neighbour, towards God. We must boldly undertake the formation of a personage for ourselves, seeking to form it in accordance with our sincerest convictions, so that it will express and show forth the person that we are.

This will no longer be a cold intellectual analysis; it will be a movement of life, a daily fashioning, a becoming, a constant adjustment of our personage in order to render it more in conformity with our thoughts, feelings and aspirations. It is an act of will, a conscious choice of an external appearance, of a line of conduct and behaviour that will be as genuine as possible.

The sincerity of the natural scene is one of the most striking and admirable things about it. Nature is beautiful because it is what it is, without any kind of affectation. We shall always wear a garment; we cannot cast it off without tearing away something of ourselves with it. What we can do is to aim at harmony, so that the garment does not belie the wearer.

One of my friends, a doctor with a gift for metaphor, was speaking to my wife about two other colleagues of ours: 'You know', he said, 'if you were to take the clothes off the one, there wouldn't be much left of him, whereas the other would weigh as much as before.'

Any dissonance between the person and the personage arouses uneasiness in us. We feel it especially in the case of hypocritical affectation, whether conscious or not. We feel it too in the case of the inner contradictions we have been discussing, from which not even the sincerest among us is free. But when the personage we show comes to the point of running counter to the quite unconscious motions of the mind, the uneasiness may take the form of obscure psychical symptoms such as anxiety, depression, obsessions and inhibitions. Such symptoms call for psychological analysis.

But the uneasiness may be the result of discordances of a quite different kind. Take, for instance, the case of a man who has missed his vocation. The social function he performs bears no relation to the essential elements of his personality, which can find no expression in it. Here the uneasiness is not a sign of disease but of health and vitality. The person stirs and struggles to burst the bonds of the personage in which it is imprisoned, like the chicken that beats with its beak against the shell of the egg that still encloses it.

The same applies to the case of a man who lives a modern life with an eighteenth-century mind. Or one who tries to act like an adult when he has remained at an infantile stage of development. One of my patients wrote to me: 'All my reactions are those of a child, but I have to hide them behind a personage which acts and speaks like a grown-up.' Another described to me a dream she had had. She had been invited out, and had put on her best frock. But when she looked in the mirror she saw that she had grown so tall that the frock was now much too short for her.

This dream expresses exactly the situation of the dreamer: she has progressed a long way along the road marked out by the discussions we have had together; she has developed towards maturity and adulthood. She is aware of an inner richness which is in contrast with the poverty of her outward life. As a matter of fact some change has already taken place in the latter, for by the grace of God she has found a more interesting and useful occupation than the one she was in before. But she has a long way to go before she reaches harmony between her social personage and her inner reality. She has an ardent nature which has been hurt many times already by dashing itself against the walls of her prison. Wisely, therefore, she tells me that she is prepared to wait now for God to make her a dress that will fit her new stature.

But in this world full concord between personage and person remains an utopian ideal. Further, by an odd paradox, we approach it only in so far as we become day by day more aware of their constant discord. So we might also say that progress in our knowledge of ourselves is progress from uneasiness to uneasiness. It is this gradual feeling our way along a road of discovery, rather than a full and complete knowledge of ourselves, which bears living fruit. The final reality of the person—always in motion, complex, mysterious and incomprehensible—still eludes us. Here and there we may catch a gleam of light, a reflection of it, just at those humbling moments when we perceive that we are not what we thought we were.

This tension that always exists between the person and the personage is one of the conditions of our life, and we must accept it. It is part of the nature of man—indeed, it is what makes him a man. Every other creature in nature is simply itself, without this discord which is our constant lot. That is why we can study everything else in nature much more surely than we can study ourselves. With ourselves, all we have to go on is an occasional glimpse of some small part of the truth, and we must be content with that, knowing that we are truly known by him who alone knows us: 'For now we see through a glass, darkly'; writes St Paul, 'but then face to face: now I know in part; but then shall I know even as also I am known' (I Cor. 13.12).

5

THE EXAMPLE OF BIOLOGY

ONE OF MY childhood memories is of being taken for the first time to a scientific lecture. I do not know how old I was—doubtless I was at the age when one is passionately interested in Jules Verne. The great hall was full to bursting; Raoul Pictet, the foremost Genevan scientist of the day, was speaking on the subject 'What is life?'

He was not one of those scientists who confine themselves to a narrow specialized field. After achieving fame through his work on artificial cold and the phenomena of very low temperatures, he devoted himself to genetical research on twins. In my young eyes, as in those of that crowded audience, he was haloed with all the prestige of science. There had even sprung up legends about him; I had been told that when he came back to Geneva he used to have magnificent baskets of flowers sent to various society ladies, but would forget to pay the bills for them. Scientists are absent-minded; perhaps that is because they occupy their minds with matters that are far above the vulgar contingencies that weigh on the common run of mortals.

Obviously I did not understand all he said, but I think the impression I received was justified: I was disappointed. I had naïvely imagined that the speaker would answer the question 'What is life?' He had told us of his experiments and his statistical investigations on the subject of twins. I had learned that there were two kinds of twins, monozygotic and dizygotic. But in spite of my youth I felt that that fell very far short of explaining life.

The scientist had properly kept to the observations he had made; my disappointment arose from the title of his address, which was very much of its day. There prevailed then a regular mystique of science, a fabulous optimism about its future. The pace of scientific discovery was increasing. What mysteries would it not in time elucidate? After the century of Newton, which had produced the explanation of physical phenomena, after that of Lavoisier and Claude Bernard, which had explained chemical phenomena in nature and physiological phenomena in living creatures, and revealed their unity, the twentieth century bade fair to pierce the secret of life and consciousness.

Since the time of Raoul Pictet biology has made great progress, but so has the modesty of the biologists; and not only of the biologists, but of all scientists. In astronomy and physics, the most rigorous of the scientific disciplines, they have been forced, first by Einstein's theory of relativity and then by Heisenberg's principle of indeterminacy, to recognize the unavoidable limits of scientific certainty, and also that the latter is concerned not with things themselves, but with the relationships between things; not reality itself but an image of reality, which is in part conventional. We might then say that it bears on the 'personage' of reality, not its 'person'.

The first principle stated by Descartes is well known: 'In order to arrive at the knowledge of all things . . . never to accept anything as true unless I know from evidence that it is so . . . and to comprehend in my judgments only that which presents itself so clearly and distinctly to my mind that I can have no occasion to doubt it.' Thereafter, until the beginning of this century, it was sincerely thought possible to separate, in the order of knowledge, the sure and certain acquisitions of science from the speculations of metaphysics. Science thus seemed like a solid edifice constructed stone by stone on unshakable foundations. Now those bases have turned out to be only hypotheses and conventions, as has been shown by Poincaré[1] and since his time by all the philosophers of science. They are no more sure and certain than the notions of metaphysics or the subjective experiences of faith.

For their part the laws of nature, which at the beginning of

[1] Henri Poincaré, *Science and Hypothesis*, Walter Scott Publishing Co., London and Newcastle-on-Tyne, 1905.

this century were still thought to be absolute, are now considered as no more than statistical laws, depending, like sociological and psychological laws, on the observer and the scale of the observation.[1]

Biologists are even more diffident. If one pursues the study of the laws which govern living phenomena—and which are subject to the same reservations as the laws of physics—one must also recognize that they cannot explain life itself. Similarly, psychology studies the laws of psychical phenomena, but that study is unable to explain the psychical fact *par excellence*, namely consciousness, which is not a phenomenon but a subjective experience. Consciousness, as Dr Tzanck explains,[2] is not a matter of knowledge, but of belief: 'You simply admit that your neighbour may, like you, be endowed with consciousness. But that is not a thing you know—you believe it. It is in fact an act of faith.'

Professor Siebeck writes: 'Science saw that it could explain many things about life, but that it could not understand life itself.'[3] Professor von Weizsäcker also recognizes the impenetrable mystery of life.[4] The doctors are joined in this by the specialist biologists, even those who, like Jean Rostand,[5] profess for science an enthusiasm which reminds one of Renan.

Firstly, the incomprehensible appearance on earth of life, like that of consciousness, constitutes the biggest gap in the scientific explanation of the world. 'One fact is certain', writes Friedel,[6] 'life, such at least as we can study scientifically, has not always existed on the earth, and it is there now.' And Jean Rostand writes:[7] 'The problem of the origin of life has not yet been satisfactorily solved.' That little word 'yet' betrays the author's

[1] Ch.-Eug. Guye, *Physico-Chemical Evolution*, translated by J. R. Clarke, Methuen & Co., London, 1925.

[2] Arnault Tzanck, *La conscience créatrice*, Charlot, Algiers, 1943.

[3] Richard Siebeck, *La vie, la maladie, le péché, la mort*, an unpublished lecture.

[4] Viktor von Weizsäcker, *Der Begriff der Allgemeinen Medizin*, Enke Verlag, Stuttgart, 1947.

[5] Jean Rostand, *La vie et ses problèmes*, Flammarion, Paris, 1939.

[6] Jean Friedel, *Biologie et foi chrétienne*, Georg, Geneva, 1942.

[7] *Op. cit.*

optimism, suggesting that the key to the mystery will some day perhaps be found.

Other biologists, like Lecomte du Noüy, have, on the contrary, very forcefully demonstrated that it is exceedingly improbable that the explanation will be found in the automatic interplay of physico-chemical phenomena alone. He bases his assertion on the work of a physicist, my teacher Charles-Eugène Guye,[1] and concludes: 'The probability for *a single* molecule of high dissymmetry to be formed by the action of chance and normal thermic agitation remains practically nil . . . we are brought to conclusion that, actually, it is *totally impossible* to account scientifically for all phenomena pertaining to life, its development and progressive evolution.'[2] And elsewhere: 'The mechanistic hypothesis is incapable of accounting for the complexity of life.'[3]

These two biologists, so different in outlook, agree also in recognizing how difficult it is even to define life. 'The problem of life has always passionately interested man. And yet there has never been a satisfactory definition of life.'[4] Jean Rostand, having recognized that it is by 'intuition' only that we oppose the world of living things to the inanimate world, continues: 'There is perhaps not one single property of living creatures which is peculiar to them alone, and which cannot also be found in an attenuated and rudimentary form in the inorganic world.'[5] He goes on to enumerate these phenomena in which specific definitions might be sought: capacity for movement, forms, organization, irritability, reactivity advantageous to self, spontaneous activity, memory, communication with the environment, birth of self, growth or assimilation. In the case of each of these phenomena he shows either that it is not certainly

[1] *Op. cit.*

[2] Lecomte du Noüy, *Human Destiny*, Longmans, Green and Co., New York, 1947, pp. 34 and 36.

[3] Lecomte du Noüy, *L'avenir de l'Esprit*, Gallimard, Paris, 1941.

[4] Lecomte du Noüy, *Biological Time*, Methuen & Co., London, 1936, p.1.

[5] *Op. cit.*

present in all living creatures, or else that it can exist apart from them.

Thus the living organism, composed of the same physical and chemical elements as the inorganic world, is also the seat of analogous physico-chemical phenomena. In a well-known passage[1] Claude Bernard puts the problem even more precisely: 'I consider that there are necessarily in the living thing two orders of phenomena: firstly, phenomena of vital creation or of organic synthesis; secondly, phenomena of death or of vital destruction. . . . The first of these two orders of phenomena is the only one without direct analogy; it is peculiar to the living being. This evolutive synthesis is the thing that is truly vital. . . . The second, on the contrary, vital destruction, is physico-chemical, usually the result of combustion, of an action comparable with a large number of chemical phenomena of decomposition or double decomposition. These, when applied to an organized being, are phenomena of death. . . .

'It is worth noting that we are here the victims of an habitual illusion; when we wish to designate phenomena of life we are really speaking of phenomena of death. The phenomena of life are not obvious to us. Organific synthesis is *internal, silent, hidden,* as to its phenomenal expression, unobtrusively assembling the materials to be expended. The phenomena of destruction or of "vital death", on the contrary, are immediately obvious to us, and it is in terms of them that we tend to identify life.' We can understand, then, Dr Tzanck's conclusion: 'All we see of life is its death.'

The reader will by now have realized the point I am leading up to. The person is also 'internal, silent, hidden', and what we see is the 'personage', the 'phenomenal expression' which is accessible to scientific study. But we must not anticipate. Let us return to Claude Bernard. Elsewhere, he has given illustrations of these two orders of phenomena: 'Take two eggs, one fertilized and the other unfertilized, and treat them both alike. One decomposes

[1] Claude Bernard, *Les phénomènes communs aux animaux et aux végétaux,* quoted by Dr Tzanck, *op. cit.*

physico-chemically, the other decomposes vitally, that is to say that the elements in one of them are used to constitute an organized body. The thing which one possesses and the other does not is vital force.'[1]

Thus the inspired physiologist was led to postulate the notion of vital force in order to explain life. It is an idea utterly foreign to science: 'It is not a fortuitous concurrence of physical and chemical phenomena which constructs each being according to a fixed and prearranged plan, and brings about the wonderful subordination and harmonious working together of the actions of life. There is in the living body an arrangement and order which cannot be overlooked, because it is indeed the most outstanding feature of living beings.'[2]

I could give many more quotations from Claude Bernard: 'It is as if a vital drawing existed which traced the plan of each organ.' 'Life is an idea ... the idea of the common result for which all the anatomical elements are associated and disciplined, the idea of the harmony which results from their combination. ... What characterizes the living machine is not the nature of its physical and chemical properties, but the creation of the machine according to a definite idea.'[3] An idea, a pattern, a plan—all these expressions imply a purposive conception of life. It is not then difficult to understand that science, which knows only causality and excludes all reference to purpose, is incapable of understanding life.

Life does not result from living phenomena; it directs them: 'The life-force directs phenomena which it does not produce; physical agents produce phenomena which they do not direct' (Claude Bernard). The whole of Lecomte du Noüy's work is a confirmation of these views: 'Our body is made up of cells, the cells of molecules, and the molecules of atoms. But these atoms are not *all* the reality of the human body. The way in which the

[1] Claude Bernard, *Le cahier rouge*, Gallimard, Paris, 1942.
[2] Maurice Vernet, *Le problème de la vie*, Plon, Paris, 1947.
[3] See A. Ferrière, *Le progrès spirituel*, Editions Forum, Geneva, 1927.

atoms, the molecules, and the cells are arranged, and which results in the unity of the individual, is also a reality, and how much more interesting.'[1]

What characterizes the living being is therefore neither its composition nor the physical and chemical phenomena which take place within it, but rather the fact that they are directed and organized. We could liken the living being to an orchestra directed by an invisible conductor. The scientist studying the orchestra and analysing each musician, can never succeed in bringing to light the secret of the harmony which results from their activity, since it is pre-established by the composer, and executed by the invisible conductor who alone knows the goal he aims at. Two wills are involved: the first is the composer who has established his plan; the second is the conductor who more or less faithfully interprets the first; the orchestra is a visible reality which to a greater or less extent obeys these two wills.

The same scheme can be applied to the subject of this book. The composer is God, who has established the plan of nature down to its minutest detail, and who has an end in view. The conductor is the invisible person, which more or less faithfully follows the plan. The orchestra is the visible personage which expresses more or less exactly the intentions of the conductor.

Coming back to biology, to crown all we find a 'purposive' expression coming from the pen of an author quite as resolutely 'mechanistic' as Jean Rostand: 'Everything takes place as if the germ contained a precision mechanism calculated to produce the final result.'[2] Life, then, is characterized not by a material function accessible to science, but by an immaterial, spiritual, purposive function. Dr Jean de Rougemont shows this to be true even of the smallest cell of the organism: it chooses from its surroundings what it is able to assimilate, and what serves to maintain life, and refuses the rest. 'Life . . . uses certain materials and disregards

[1] Lecomte du Noüy, *Biological Time*, p. 32.
[2] Maurice Vernet, *op. cit.*

the remainder. It thus makes a choice . . . feeling, or rather sensitivity. . . . In this constant selection there is clearly an element of memory and also of intelligence.'[1]

Dr Tzanck, trained in the discipline of the laboratory and the doctrines of materialist science, describes[2] how he came to recognize these two immaterial conceptions of choice and memory as indispensable to an understanding of life: 'It is as if the tissue itself were able to recognize a particular agent. . . . In this "specific" reaction it is not difficult to see all the characteristics proper to mnemonic phenomena.' What he calls 'creative consciousness' can plainly be identified with what I call the person in this book, an intangible, invisible, yet fundamental reality, from which life flows forth, and the effects of which we perceive indirectly in the tangible reality which is accessible to scientific study.

Again, Dr Jean de Rougemont, speaking of life, says: 'Like electricity, no one has ever seen it, or laid hands on it. We observe electrical phenomena, we also observe living phenomena.' Dr Maurice Vernet has expressed the same idea: he sees in the living being 'the fundamental characteristic of obedience to will which implies essentially a choice'. Moreover, 'there takes place a kind of adaptation of the response to the stimulus, an adaptation which has the features of a phenomenon of memory'.[3]

The last-mentioned author takes us even further into the analysis of the mechanisms of life. 'The basic equilibrium which characterizes life', he writes, 'is revealed in the constancy of the composition of the tissues and protoplasm, in the stability of the metabolic rate, in the interdependence of bodily rhythms, in the harmony of functions. . . . Equilibrium involves regulation.' The essential and characteristic function which ensures this regulation in all living cells Dr Vernet calls 'organic sensitivity'.[4]

[1] Jean de Rougemont, *Vie du corps et vie de l'esprit*, Paul Derain, Lyons, 1945.
[2] *Op. cit.*
[3] *Op. cit.*
[4] Maurice Vernet, *La sensibilité organique*, Flammarion, Paris, 1948.

Life

This regulation is not rigid, but flexible. There is no life without fluctuation, without incessant oscillations about a mean equilibrium. Fixity is death. Thus the composition of protoplasm is constant only on an average; it varies continually from the average. That is why it is so difficult in medicine to determine the frontier between the normal and the pathological. The pathological is a deviation beyond the margin within which deviation is normal.

To sum up, what characterizes the living being, when compared with the inorganic world, is this constant instability which is nevertheless manifestly controlled by a regulator, by a directing thought, since in the normal state the extent of the oscillation is always limited. It is as if a mysterious unseen will were engaged in conducting this complex organism in a chosen direction, constantly bringing back on to its course each element the moment it deviates from it.

In the analogy of the orchestra, just now, I said that it 'more or less' obeys its conductor, and he the composer. It is when the double-basses play too loudly that the conductor signals to them to play more softly. Thus the harmony that results is an approximation, based on the incessant correction of incipient disharmonies. This is exactly what we have just noted in the case of the living being—constant slight deviations by each of its elements and at the same time a will which rectifies them immediately in order to carry into effect a preconceived plan.

Let us take a different image. The inorganic world may be compared to a train which is compelled by the rigid rails on which it runs to follow exactly a pre-established course. The world of living things, on the other hand, is like a motor-car which enjoys a certain margin of deviation from side to side on the road. Its course is kept practically straight by means of continual corrections to right or left applied through the steering wheel. Without this regulation the car would finish up in the ditch. But the regulation is a supple one, needing an intelligent driver, not an inflexible rail.

Claude Bernard himself wrote: 'The organism is regarded as a machine, and that is right; but it is considered as a fixed, immovable, automatic machine, confined within precise mathematical limits, and that is quite wrong. The organism is an organic machine, endowed, that is to say, with a flexible, elastic mechanism.' So, compared with the inorganic world, the living being enjoys a certain margin of deviation from the line of its course, and it is just this which makes it a living being. Its life is maintained by these perpetual fluctuations, regulated by organic sensitivity. We shall see later that man enjoys a still wider margin of deviation than the animals, and again it is just this which makes him a man.

We are touching here on a problem that is very difficult to explain, but one which seems to me to be of the first importance for an understanding of the relationship that exists between the personage and the person. Let us return once again to our motorist. If he is accustomed to driving, he controls the progress of his vehicle quite automatically, through acquired reflexes. But when he arrives at a cross-roads, his action in turning the steering-wheel to take the road on the left or the right is of quite a different sort. He exercises his will to make a conscious decision.

Thus we have the same driver, making the same movement with his steering-wheel, but this time the significance of his action is of quite a different order. In the first case his action is automatic and recurrent; in the second it is an isolated act of the will. So in the life of man, what is seen, what is observable scientifically, is what is automatic—the personage. For science knows nothing of the unique fact; it can deduce laws only from facts which recur again and again. I refer of course to natural science, which differs in this from the science of history. But even history becomes a science only in so far as the historian compares recurrent facts. Apart from that it is only a collection of unique facts, and therefore unintelligible.

We can understand then how it is that the person always eludes objective investigation, that it is always only the personage that one finds. Science comprehends only the automatic aspects of the living being, which thus appears to it to be nothing more than a collection of automatic phenomena.

It seems therefore that life is composed of two distinct elements, corresponding to Claude Bernard's two orders of phenomena: the first, which is proper only to life, is creative, unique, instantaneous, purposive, metaphysical, and inaccessible to scientific observation; it is the turn of the steering-wheel at the cross-roads, turning the car in the chosen direction. The second is automatic, recurrent, lasting, causal, physical, and alone accessible to science; it is the automatic correction which serves to keep the vehicle on the course on which it has been set.

Dr Tzanck gives a telling illustration of this conception of life, drawn from the field of evolution. It is well known that the doctrine of transformism, after its tremendous initial success, has had to be abandoned. It arose out of an intuitive feeling that there was a natural kinship between the different species. This view necessarily implied that 'living beings were capable of acquiring new characteristics and of transmitting them to their descendants. . . . Now, not only has no irrefutable proof of such natural transformations ever been forthcoming, but also every attempt to create a hereditarily transmissible mutilation in an organism has failed.'[1]

In other words, the creative phenomenon is always outside the purview of science. Science observes only the automatic phenomena which tend, on the contrary, to uphold 'the fixity of the species against the idea of evolution'. Dr Tzanck therefore concludes: 'It is as if at the origin of each adaptation there arose a possibility of choice, a consciousness. It is as if conscious acquisitions were remembered and repeated automatically by the living matter. Of these two kinds of facts, one of adaptation, the other of repetition, only the second is accessible to our knowledge.'

You will see that this biologist's conclusions correspond very closely to our analogy of the motorist. He eluded us at that brief instant when he chose his new route at the cross-roads. But the

[1] *Op. cit.*

fact that he did choose it is obvious, for there he is, travelling along it. Once again, as he travels, we are able to observe the automatic reflexes by means of which he keeps his vehicle going in the new direction, as if his body preserved the memory of it.

The essential, creative, personal act of life eludes our observation; all we see is the automatic action which prolongs that primary act, and which has no longer anything specifically living about it. This automatic activity ensures the fixity of the individual as well as of the species. It makes him a personage. To the person belongs free choice, everything that is not fixed and automatic. But the choice is made manifest only by the continuing automatic action which it has set going. We can understand now why we could not detach the personage from the person, why the person was not directly accessible to us. We were able to trace it only through a personage which was already more or less firmly set in the role it played, already more or less deprived of liberty and life.

This automatic action is therefore a witness of life, but also a negation of it. It is at one and the same time its constant fruit, its indispensable servant, and its grave.

Firstly, its constant fruit: This is what I showed in Chapter 4 —the impossibility of separating the person from the personage, of living at every moment an original and spontaneous life. The fabric of our existence is woven from end to end with these automatisms: physiological, psychological, moral and spiritual as well, they serve to give a certain continuity to our being. Dr Tzanck writes that even in our own selves it is 'difficult to distinguish consciousness from the automatisms it has created'.

Often I see people who are obsessed with this search for a quite personal originality. They want to be really themselves, to break away from all the determining factors of their bodies, their heredity, their complexes, reflexes, and upbringing. They resist every external influence, for fear of losing their personality. They want to owe nothing to anyone, have only original thoughts, and feelings which no one has experienced before.

In the result, however, this turning in upon themselves, depriving them of fruitful intercourse with other people, impoverishes their lives and their personalities. What is left of us if we take away everything borrowed from outside and everything that partakes of the nature of habit within us? A gaping void. I once put it to one of these people like this: we do not do embroidery in the empty air, but on a piece of material. This material is like the network of automatisms, without which there would would be no being, no life, no possibility of embroidery—that is to say, of personal creative activity.

This brings me to my second point about these automatic actions, that they are, in fact, the necessary servants of life. If my 'creative consciousness' had to attend every moment to the functioning of each of my cells, each of my organs, to the secretions of all my glands, it would have no time left for the writing of these lines! Automatisms are an economy of consciousness. Our motorist could converse with his wife at the same time as he drove his car by means of acquired reflexes. Just for a moment at the cross-roads he broke off the conversation to give his attention to the road and the sign-post.

In a masterly book[1] Dr Paul Cossa describes this hierarchy of the nervous system 'from the reflex to the psychical'. He shows that whereas the science of anatomy has precisely located the centres of the lower, concrete functions of sense and motor activity, the higher, more abstract functions of intelligence have not been localized at all. And that the strictly automatic nature of the lower functions makes possible 'the progressive liberation of nervous activity from attention to the bodily activities which sustain it'.

Our organs actually work much better when we leave them to their automatic functioning and do not think about them. That this is so is clearly shown in the case of the hypochondriac, who suffers from all kinds of functional disorders simply because his mind occupies itself with his body. These disorders attract the attention of his mind, and thus he is caught in a vicious circle.

[1] Paul Cossa, *Du réflexe au psychique*, Desclée de Brouwer, Bruges, 1948.

His preoccupation with himself develops in its turn into an automatism so powerful that he reaches a stage at which he is incapable of thinking of anything but his own ills.

Lastly, these automatic actions are also the tomb of life. When we say of someone that he has an extremely lively personality, we mean that he is full of creative imagination, of unexpected caprices, and unforeseen whims. All this is the very opposite of automatic—those humdrum lives I have been describing in this book seem already dead before their time, before physiological death arrests the working of the mechanisms of body and mind which are, so to speak, the only things left alive in them.

The liveliness of the child comes of his not yet having, like the adult, been subjected to the inexorable mould of automatism. His spontaneity is contagious: he makes us feel freer, as if the too close-fitting garment which was constricting us has been loosened. And when a man becomes set in a rigid mode of thought and habit, we feel that he has grown prematurely old, that life is being extinguished in him. He always repeats the same formulae of word and action. His reaction to every situation can be foreseen. He is nothing more than a well-trained animal.

Indeed, it is not what is really human, but the merely animal in us that is automatic. This is incontestably the case with the all-powerful working of our instincts; it is also true of the conditioned reflexes implanted in us by education and habit; but even the so-called spiritual archetypes, described by the School of C. G. Jung, to which, without knowing it, we are subject, although they may in certain respects distinguish us from the animals, do, by their automatic character, nevertheless recall the nature of the animal.

In the animal everything is automatic. I can see this clearly in my dog: the moment my game of chess is finished, he gets up and comes over to me, for it is time for his little walk. In psychology our scientific study can be done on animals, because it is concerned only with what we have in common with them, not so much with our actions as with our reactions, our natural and acquired reflexes.

There can be no question of denying the animal in us, of disowning this highly developed machine which reacts perfectly adequately to every stimulus. It is the mainstay of our existence. But if that is all there is in me, I am not a man. Love, for example, in so far as it can be studied scientifically, is merely a natural function. Whether it be the sex instinct, the maternal instinct, or simple emotional states, or the need to love and be loved, which the animal feels as much as we do, these are still nothing more than automatic reactions to external stimuli.

But when love suddenly springs up when we least expect it—love for a hostile individual substituted for the natural aggressive riposte, prompting forgiveness, displacing self-interest—then we are in the presence of a creative act that is really free and undetermined. It is a bursting forth of life, a positive choosing of a new direction, breaking the chain of natural reactions.

This is action properly so called, truly spontaneous and creative, and as such it remains isolated, unique and unforeseeable—and so impossible to study scientifically. It is a manifestation of the person thrusting aside the personage. But it will become in its turn the source of a new set of automatic reactions to a multitude of situations, reactions which will be accessible to the objective examination of psychology. They will be the evidence of the new force that is at work, just as we may be certain that there is a locomotive drawing the line of waggons we can see moving on the horizon, even though it may be hidden from view.

We have here a picture of these two inseparable aspects of life: the force which we cannot see, and the train of automatisms behind it, which we do see. But the line of waggons is not life in its essence, the person; it is purely passive, a dead thing. This new set of automatisms which we have just been discussing, started by a living spiritual event, will, by dint of repetition, gradually lose their deep significance, and, taking on the character of habits, become part of the personage. Born from a bursting forth of life, they will wither, unless rekindled by fresh creative acts, into a deadening routine.

It would seem that the same is true of organic life. Dr Tzanck quotes two sayings by Claude Bernard: 'Life is creation', and 'Life is death'. There is, he says, no contradiction here. 'Life is at one and the same time both creation and death: creation in its inner unseen existence—death in its visible manifestations.'[1]

Of course we are here making, in order to understand them, a distinction between these two aspects of life that is too clear-cut. In reality they are intimately bound up together. Moment by moment our life is made up of the death of each of our cells. These 'phenomena of death' of which Claude Bernard spoke, these cellular disintegrations, which are purely physico-chemical phenomena, and the only ones accessible to scientific observation, are taking place within us while we live—and we should not be living if they were not taking place. It is the same with our mental life, in which the complexes and the spontaneous associations of ideas studied by the psychologists are comparable in every respect with the phenomena of cellular chemistry. Our personal life is thus indissolubly bound up with the life of our tissues. Let the latter be disturbed, and we find ourselves incapable of making a creative decision.

But life is much more than that. Amid the inexorable monotony of all these observable mechanisms it resurges continually in the secret depths of our being, as if intermittent explosions were breaking the bonds of the automatisms which it has itself set in motion. In the same way the person can transfigure the petrified routine of the personage and give it a new complexion.

'Consciousness', writes Dr Tzanck, 'does not repeat, it imagines.' And again: 'True thought is thought alone.'[2] So every creative event, every resurgence of life, comes to upset the established order of the routine automatisms, but it immediately gives rise to new ones, which take the place of the old. It would seem then that there is a sort of rhythm of life between its stereotyped forms, which are alone observable, and the intangible pulsations which save it from imprisonment within them. The person is manifested in these intermittent flashes, whereas all that is continuous in us is personage.

[1] *Op. cit.*   [2] *Op. cit.*

The painter Corot spent the early part of his career laboriously groping after the form of expression that suited him. But having found it he became its prisoner: 'He paints Corots because that is what people demand of him.'[1] From then on, Corot evolved no more; he became fixed in a set personage. Life is movement, the breaking of the fixed line, instability. That is the great consolation that we can give to those who suffer from nervous disorders, when they complain of their instability of temperament. The perfectly stable being is nothing but an automaton, without life—a thing. We have come back here to the notion of a margin of fluctuation which, as I have already pointed out, is characteristic of life.

We have come back also to the old distinction made by philosophers between *Natura naturans* and *Natura naturata:* life is both the creative origin of nature and the natural created state which we study. The former eludes us, just as substances in the 'nascent state' of the chemists elude us; for as soon as they appear during chemical reaction they combine at once with other substances.

Similarly, the analysis of an internal combustion engine cannot explain to us why it is going; for an impulse from outside was necessary to start up the cycle of automatic reactions which is taking place within it, and which is thus perpetuating the original movement imparted to it.

We can understand now Bergson's well-known assertion:[2] 'The intellect is characterized by a natural inability to comprehend life.' Or, as he puts it elsewhere: 'Intelligence . . . is able to comprehend only bodies that are discontinuous and inert. It is incapable of grasping life in its continuity and its progress.' He echoes the Oriental wisdom of Confucius: 'We know not what life is.' We can understand too Professor Gusdorf's remark: 'In short, we try to track down the ego, but all we ever find is the products it leaves in its wake.'[3] Life, the ego, the person, are not

[1] Georges Gusdorf, *La découverte de soi.*

[2] Henri Bergson, *Creative Evolution*, translated by Arthur Mitchell, Macmillan & Co., London, 1911, p. 174.

[3] *La découverte de soi.*

palpable, analysable realities accessible to science. They are a will, a choice, a consciousness, an impulse coming from another, metaphysical sphere, of which we see only the indirect effect in the physico-chemical sphere. 'The essence of life remains outside our grasp', writes Dr Ponsoye, because 'it is beyond human power, and lies in the intangible supernatural' (Professor H. Rouvière).[1]

[1] Pierre Ponsoye, *L'esprit, force biologique fondamentale*, Imprimerie Causse, Graille & Castelnau, Montpellier, 1942.

6

PSYCHOLOGY AND SPIRIT

THESE CONCLUSIONS will of course be unacceptable to those of my colleagues who have decided arbitrarily to exclude from medicine all reference to metaphysics. They sincerely believe that in this they are being more objective than I. They may justly impute to me a preconceived idea: that of the believer convinced that the origin of the world, the source of life and of consciousness, lies outside this tangible world, in a free and creative will which he calls God; convinced that the person, that which distinguishes man from the animal, is also an invisible reality 'in the image of God' (Gen. 1.27). But I am also entitled to see in them another preconceived idea, that of the positivism which admits no other reality than that which is accessible to scientific study.

I do not suppose that rational debate would bring us to agreement. I have confined myself to showing that, in its present state at least, positivist science is unable to explain life. I am the first to recognize that in concluding that life and the person are of a spiritual order we can only suppose or believe it, not demonstrate it.

Nevertheless the analogy between the problem of life and that of the person is striking. It is probably not fortuitous that they both remain mysteries, and that we perceive only their indirect effects. Biology does seem to me to have something important to teach us concerning the problem of the person. I am not only a psychologist; I am a doctor, of the body as well as the mind, and I mean to remain such. It seems to me that psychologists who are not doctors necessarily lack an element which is important in forming judgments. Anatomy and physiology are still the fundamental bases of knowledge about man. Throughout our lives we remain dependent on our bodies, and can only develop within the limits they set us.

Whether we speak of an idea, of a vital drawing or a life force, with Claude Bernard, of the *élan vital* with Bergson, or of creative consciousness with Dr Tzanck, we are referring, in order to explain life, to a spiritual power, external to the tangible world but imparting to it a movement which we can detect with our senses. I do not claim to demonstrate this hidden reality, since in fact it eludes objective investigation. But I do claim that it is the only satisfactory explanation of the phenomena we observe in biology. We are led, then, to the concept of an invisible spiritual power which animates the visible world of living things.

This is precisely the conception we find in the Bible. The creative power is God, the divine Word which calls first the inorganic world into existence, and then the biological world to life: 'The Lord God formed man of the dust of the ground, and breathed into his nostrils the breath of life; and man became a living soul' (Gen. 2.7). And St Paul, on the Areopagus in Athens, announces the 'God that made the world and all things therein', who, he adds, is 'not far from every one of us: for in him we live, and move, and have our being' (Acts 17.24, 27 and 28).

I should like to show the reader how this conception resolves, in medical thought, difficulties which without it seem absolutely insurmountable. Let us consider our orchestra again. There are in an orchestra two big principal groups of instruments, strings and wind. We may compare them to the two constituent elements of the living being, the body and the mind. By the mind I mean the ψυχή, studied by the psychologists.

The invisible conductor of the orchestra controls both these groups of instruments at the same time, and co-ordinates them. He makes a sign first to the one and then to the other to take up the principal theme, in accordance with the plan laid down by the composer. Similarly in a sick person our attention is drawn now by physical and now by psychical symptoms, but the two kinds are always there.

Without the invisible conductor the astonishing correlation which exists between the organic facts and the psychical facts remains an impenetrable mystery. For example, I am sad (a psychical sign) and I weep (a physical sign). On what does the correlation between these two signs rest? I may think, with certain doctors, that I weep because I am sad (the psychogenic interpretation). But that leaves the mechanism unexplained: why does my sadness provoke secretion in my lachrymal glands rather than contraction of my big toe? I may think, with other doctors, that I experience the sensation of sadness because my lachrymal glands are secreting tears—and of course, because at the same time all sorts of other mechanisms are at work in my vegetative nervous system—(the organicist interpretation). But in this case there is no explanation of why these nervous phenomena are accompanied by a feeling of sadness rather than of joy.

In every case the argument between the partisans of the psychogenic interpretation and those of the organicist interpretation remains sterile. The only thing we can be sure of is that the two symptoms occur together. It is impossible to prove that one controls the other, or, again, that both are controlled, as I am maintaining here, by an invisible conductor, the person. Especially is psychiatry deeply divided into two enemy camps, the upholders of the psychogenic interpretation and those of the organicist interpretation. I am often classed with the former; I absolutely refuse to agree. For me it is neither the body which controls the mind, nor the mind which controls the body; rather are both at once the expression of an invisible reality of a spiritual order—the person.

In referring to tears I was taking a very simple example in order to make my point clear. But the same problem crops up throughout the whole field of medicine. From Hippocrates onwards, doctors have always been passionately interested in these psycho-physical concordances, without any satisfactory explanation to them, from the purely scientific point of view, having been found. Kretschmer has shown the concordance between certain types of physique and a predisposition to certain mental diseases, for example the pyknic type to manic-depressive psychosis. Even without having made a study of physiognomy, we all judge from a cursory glance at our neighbour's face whether he is an anxious type or a contented one, profound or superficial.

Does the mind mould the body, or is it the body which determines the mind? No one can say with certainty. Professor Georgi has recently taken up the question again in connection with the chemical analysis of the blood. 'This psycho-physical correlation', he writes, 'is a mystery to us.' He adds: 'Our psychical and bodily existence is subject to a rhythm of its own, the modulation of which appears to be determined by the Mind.'[1]

Most doctors scarcely give a thought to these disturbing and fundamental questions. They are practical people who, according to the circumstances of the case, make either an organic or a psychogenic interpretation. In regard to each case with which they have to deal they ask themselves, either explicitly or implicitly, this question—is it organic or functional? If physical medicines do not succeed, they say to themselves: 'This must be nervous.' And if psychotherapy fails, they think: 'It must be organic.'

Thus, medicine as I was taught it supposed that there were two fundamentally distinct classes of disease, the organic and the functional. This idea has always worried me. Are not all organic diseases accompanied by functional disturbances? Moreover, as Dr Abrami has pointed out, the latter play a much greater part than that played by the lesions in giving such cases their 'differing countenances'.[2] And is not every functional disease accompanied by physical symptoms?

Furthermore, the American psychosomatic school of medicine has shown us that a serious organic lesion, such as a stomach ulcer, in which classical medicine saw the first cause of the disease, may

[1] F. Georgi, 'Psychophysische Korrelationen', in *Schweizerische Medizinische Wochenschrift*, 1948, No. 23, p. 553.

[2] See Georges Menkès, *Médecine sans frontières*, Editions du Mont-Blanc, Geneva, 1945.

on the contrary be its final stage, following upon years of purely functional and psychogenic disturbances. Professor Leriche has, in numerous publications, likewise set us thinking along more synthetic lines. He shows how a 'surgical' organic lesion—ankylosis of the hip—has had the ground silently prepared for it by years of very minor disturbances in the tissues, having nothing specific about them. 'Disease', he writes, 'is like a drama whose first acts have been played before the lights have gone up on the stage.'[1]

It seems then that we must forsake this division between organic diseases and functional diseases, and substitute for it a quite different notion; namely, that every disease shows itself in both physical and psychical disturbances at the same time, but that these are more or less reversible. The constant fluctuations of our physiology, of which I spoke earlier, are not only functional, but also organic, since they result in differing analyses in the laboratory, shadows on the X-ray photograph, or variations under the microscope. But they remain reversible as long as the regulative activity of organic sensitivity continues.

The greater the amplitude of these fluctuations, or the more they are repeated, the less reversible they become. It is then what we call a 'lesion'; would it not be better to call it a 'scar'? The body is less supple than the mind, as the brass in the orchestra is less supple than the strings. When these lesions lose their reversibility, their aptitude for regeneration, they become fixed, and automatic regulation disappears. Our motorist, too, would drive into the ditch if his steering-wheel became locked.

Clearly, such a conception of man is infinitely more satisfying to the mind than a purely organicist or a purely psychogenic conception, or again one that is alternatively organicist and psychogenic. According to it, it is a spiritual impulsion, man's spiritual destiny, which controls both his bodily and his mental phenomena, whether normal or pathological. The body and the

[1] René Leriche, 'Qu'est-ce que la maladie?', in *Journal de médecine de Bordeaux et du Sud-Ouest*, October, 1950.

mind are only the means of expression of the spirit, which co-ordinates and directs them both at once. The body and the mind which we study both appear simply as mechanisms, therefore as personages, the instruments by means of which the spiritual reality which is the person expresses itself.

Recently, in Scandinavia, my colleagues spoke to me about the work of Dr Huebschmann, which has already been severely criticized by a noted Norwegian specialist in tuberculosis. Dr Huebschmann[1] has undertaken the psychological analysis of a large number of tuberculosis patients, and has shown that the evolutive phases of the disease regularly coincide with periods during which the mind is troubled by serious inner conflicts, particularly moral conflicts. The Scandinavian specialist had apparently protested against this tendency to give a systematic 'psychological interpretation' of cases of organic disease.

Now it seems to me that there is a grave confusion here. For my part, I do not see in Dr Huebschmann's work a 'psychological interpretation' of tuberculosis, but rather a spiritual one, which is quite a different matter. A serious conflict of conscience is not merely a psychological fact, it is an intimate spiritual event which expresses itself in two ways at once—in the psychical manifestations which Dr Huebschmann studies by means of analysis, and in the physical symptoms revealed to him by auscultation and radiography.

A woman suffering from tuberculosis came to consult me last year. She had been for more than four years under the excellent care of a noted tuberculosis specialist. She had first suggested coming to consult me two years previously, but he had dissuaded her. 'Dr Tournier treats nervous diseases', he had said, 'you are tubercular!' But she had broached the subject again last year when her doctor had once more ordered her to spend the winter in the mountains. And, paradoxically, I myself at first refused to treat her, so great is my fear of seeing the indispensable

[1] Heinri Huebschmann, *Psyche und Tuberkulose*, Ferdinand Enke Verlag, Stuttgart, 1952.

measures for care of the body being neglected under the pretext of treating the mind.

But the woman was so insistent, both with her own doctor and with me, that I at last agreed with him to take her on. This woman had psychological troubles which my colleague had naturally been unable to detect either by auscultation or by radiography: a desertion complex and an inferiority complex, due to childhood experiences. In addition there were moral problems: a Roman Catholic, she had contracted a second marriage with a divorced Protestant, and that had estranged her from her Church. Lastly there were other conflicts, particularly concerning the children of her husband's first marriage.

But very soon she opened her heart to me more deeply still. And so we gradually passed from psychology to the realm of the spirit. During adolescence, while at a Catholic boarding-school, she had formed an association with a schoolmate from abroad who was passionately addicted to the reading of Nietzsche. She herself was still immature mentally, incapable of holding her own in argument with a stronger mind. She was soon convinced that the religion she had been taught was nothing but an illusion. Thereafter, she was no longer able to pray; she even found it impossible at the time of the tragic death of her first husband. She felt that she lacked something, but had never found anyone to whom she could talk about it.

Following on our conversation, she found her Catholic faith again. I remember that when she came back for her second consultation her face was radiant, and she told me that she was praying again. She added jokingly that in the evening when her husband, a hard-worked factory manager, was late home, instead of working herself into a state of nervous impatience she found it was an excellent opportunity for saying her prayers! From that time the condition of her lungs rapidly improved. Four months later my colleague was able to announce that she was cured of tuberculosis.

This case is a good illustration of this fundamental problem of the relationship of soul, mind and body. I certainly do not say that she was suffering from a 'psychogenic tuberculosis'. I do say that there existed a spiritual problem which compromised at the same time both her physical and her mental health, with the result that my colleague found physical symptoms, and I found psychical symptoms.

It is true that we were led into the domain of the spiritual along the road of psychology, because psychology is more conducive to personal contact than are auscultation and radiography. But truth to tell, there was nothing very scientific about the psychology I used in this case. I do not remember having done any analysis of dreams. All I did was to listen to that woman just as any general practitioner might after having sounded her chest.

Thinking it over, one realizes that every psychotherapist sooner or later goes beyond the strictly psychological sphere—even the Freudians, in spite of their principles. The recounting of a life-story, a mind thinking aloud, freed from the bonds of formalism, leads one inevitably to the consideration of problems which are no longer psychological but spiritual, problems such as the meaning of life and of the world, of disease and of death, of sin and of faith, or one's own scale of values. Dr Igor Caruso has, I think, very clearly defined this inevitable passage of the psychotherapist from the technical and analytic to the synthetic and 'existential'.[1]

The reader will see the great importance of the distinction I make here between the domain of psychology and that of the spiritual life. Psychology is a science, a method, a technique, which lays bare the mechanisms of the mind. But as soon as there is any question, in the course of treatment, of the patient's attitude to himself or to others, towards life and towards God, we have left the technical sphere for that of morality and metaphysics. The doctor at that point is no longer engaged in psychotherapy, but in soul-healing.

I have sometimes been accused of not recognizing the frontier between these two, and of being in danger of confusing them. It

[1] Igor A. Caruso, *Psychanalyse und Synthese der Existenz*, Herder, Vienna, 1952.

seems to me that the real danger is that of mixing them without realizing it, and not in intermingling them openly and consciously as I do. For in practice all psychotherapists do intermingle them. The one who does not recognize the frontier is in fact the one who sincerely believes himself to be still a psychotherapist, and who claims to continue himself to the scientific sphere of psychology, when actually he has entered the field of soul-healing.

The psychotherapist who suggests, naïvely enough, that as part of his therapeutic treatment his patient should indulge in a 'sexual adventure' outside marriage, is not at that point engaging in psychotherapy, but in soul-healing—a soul-healing inspired by his own theology, which makes a god of the instincts. To those doctors and theologians who ask me whether it is right for the doctor to enter the domain of the spiritual, foreign to medicine in their view, I must reply with another question: 'What soul-healing is he practising? On what theology, on what conception of the world and of man is it based?'

But the frontier is difficult to define; one crosses it imperceptibly. In a recent article,[1] I showed this to be so with regard to each of the four basic functions of the psychotherapist. Firstly, in 'catharsis', after the patient has spoken of all those things of which he has been the victim, he always turns to those things for which he feels he is to blame. The problem of sin is raised, and at the same time that of grace, which is the only answer. We are no longer in the technical sphere.

And then, in 'transference': as Dr Maeder has shown,[2] there is more in this than an affective phenomenon, there is personal contact, communion, an event of a spiritual nature. Thirdly, as the patient comes to self-knowledge, the more clearly he sees himself, the more aware does he become of that tangle of contradictions we have described, of man's powerlessness to realize his true aspirations. Then it is no longer of healing alone that he

[1] Paul Tournier, 'The Frontier between Psychotherapy and Soul-Healing', in *Journal of Psychotherapy as a Religious Process*, No. 1, Dayton, Ohio, January, 1954.

[2] A. Maeder, *La personne du médecin, un agent psychothérapeutique*, Delachaux and Niestlé, Neuchâtel. 1953.

stands in need, but of Salvation, of the assurance that the world and he have been redeemed.

Finally the psychotherapist, as we have just seen, inevitably exercises a philosophical function. This deep exploring of the mind necessarily leads to the raising of questions to which technique has no answer. Even if the psychotherapist does not furnish an answer, on principles of strict spiritual neutrality, he must by his whole attitude exert an influence on his patient in this field. This influence is not psychotherapeutic in the true sense, but spiritual. It does not depend on the technique he uses, but on his own person, on his own view of the world, on his own faith. This, moreover, is true of every doctor, including even the surgeon, for they all have a moral influence on their patients.

Psychoanalysts themselves are coming more and more to realize this. In all his most recent writings Dr Maeder has had much to say on the subject. Among the various schools which have come into being as a result of Freud's discoveries, it seems that it is that of Rank which has best understood the close connection between psychology and spiritual life. Characteristic of this trend is the new American *Journal of Psychotherapy as a Religious Process*, published by the Rank Institute in Dayton, Ohio.

But I recall a remark made by Dr Kütemeyer, which I have quoted elsewhere: 'The soul is no nearer the mind than it is to the body.' Spiritual life involves the whole person, and not only the psychological processes studied by the psychologists. Dr Maeder writes:[1] 'Faith is essentially the affair of the person.' And Dr A. Stocker:[2] 'It is the spiritual which makes the person.' If the frontier between psychology and the life of the spirit is hard to define, nevertheless in crossing it we enter a completely different domain, that of judgments of values, of faith, of decisions involving self-commitment—in a word, we are in the domain of the person, and no longer in that of the automatic psychical

[1] A. Maeder, *Vers la guérison de l'âme.*
[2] A. Stocker, 'Structures affectives ou hiérarchie de la personne', in *Archivio di Psicologia, Neurologia e Psichiatria, Anno X Fasc. III*, September, 1949, Milan.

mechanisms. And the fortunes of this spiritual life are manifested in the body as much as in the mind.

In this world the action of the soul is observable only in physical and psychical phenomena determined by it; in a loss or a renewal of vitality, in moods, feelings and thoughts. It is the source of considerable difficulties, for when the body or the mind are disturbed, they put a false colouring on the spiritual life. Thus people suffering from depression are beset by false feelings of guilt; they mistake for matters of conscience things that are only the effect of psychical disturbances. If we look through red glass we get the impression that the whole scene is red.

Also, it is always through a personage that we approach the person—through the physical personage of organic medicine, or through the psychological personage studied by scientific psychology. Thus physique, physiognomy, chirology and all the ups and downs of the body are sources of information about the person, as also are psychological complexes and tests. Perhaps the reader is surprised that I have not mentioned the latter before now. It is not because I do not recognize their value.

I make use especially of Jung's original test, based on the free association of ideas provoked by words. I also use the best-known of them, the Rorschach test, based on the free association of ideas provoked by the odd shapes made by ink-blots compressed between the sides of a folded piece of paper. I understand that Szondi's tests are even more fertile in the results they give, but I am not yet acquainted with them. No one, of course, could give a complete list of all the tests in existence, since anyone can invent for himself as many as he likes, and base a whole technique upon them.

But it is clear that tests, like every other scientific technique, lead only indirectly to the person. They reach only the personage directly. By their very nature they reveal only automatisms. Their value lies precisely in the fact that they bring to light the subject's reactions freed as far as possible from the control of reason, consciousness and will. The most one can say is that they are a means of studying the personality. The personality lies between the person and the personage, since it comprises innate characteristics and everything that has been added to them by education and life.[1] But it pertains to the order of the personage, as I have defined it in this book, for it is comprised only of automatisms. In the same way, all the mechanisms studied by psychology— complexes, repressions, projections, archetypes—are, strictly speaking, only automatisms. Likewise, also, the conditioned reflexes of the School of Pavlov. All this reminds us of what the Romans used to say of man: *non agit, sed agitur* (he does not act, he is acted upon). All these methods furnish us with useful and valid evidence concerning man, but about only one aspect of him, and that the least human: his automatic aspect. In a recent lecture Dr Mitscherlich declared that modern psychology was in danger of reducing the destiny of man to a sort of mechanism, and so of depriving psychical phenomena of their personal aspect.[2]

We have in fact seen that depth psychology can be a wonderful road towards personal contact, towards an awakening of spiritual life. For it draws the doctor away from his position of cold intellectual objectivity. 'Psychoanalysis', writes Professor von Weizsäcker, 'has introduced the subjective into psychopathology.'[3] But it is capable also, through an excessive generalization of its doctrines when it claims to be a complete explanation of man, of depersonalizing him, treating him as an absolutely automatic machine, with no more free will than Buridan's donkey.

Nevertheless, even a Freudian like Dr Charles Odier[4] is able

[1] Translator's note: Cf. Professor James Drever's definition: 'It would appear in the main to comprise the natural and acquired impulses and habits, interests and complexes, the sentiments and ideals, the opinions and beliefs, as manifested in the individual's relations with his social milieu.' *A Dictionary of Psychology*, Penguin Books, Harmondsworth, 1952.

[2] Alexander Mitscherlich, 'Neue Ergebnisse in der wissenschaftlichen Weltorientierung'. Conference on Psychotherapy and Psychosomatic Medicine Cf. *Neue Zürcher Zeitung*, Zurich, No. 741.

[3] Cf. Alphonse Maeder, *Le rôle du contact affectif en psychothérapie*, address delivered at the International Congress on Psychotherapy, Leyden, 1951.

[4] Charles Odier, *Les deux sources consciente et inconsciente de la vie morale*, La Baconnière, Neuchâtel, 1943.

to make the distinction (which Freud himself did not make) between 'functions' and 'values'. The 'functions' are the automatisms studied by psychology. The 'values' are of the order of the person, of a spiritual order; they elude psychological study.

It remains for me to show that our spiritual life itself also presents the double aspect I have described: it is made up of intermittent creative flashes and permanent automatisms. In art, too, we find the same mixture: a work of art springs from a creative inspiration, but it can be manifested only through a technique, that is to say through acquired automatisms.

The religious life itself is no different in this respect. Point by point we shall find in it all the features we have noted above with regard to life: the incessant fluctuations, regulations and sensitivity, the elusive and intermittent character of that which is specifically living and creative, and lastly the automatisms which prolong it, and which are at one and the same time its witnesses, its support and its tomb.

Firstly, the fluctuations: many of the people I see yearn for a stable spiritual life. They blame themselves, after bursts of fervour, for falling back into lukewarmness, and after victories of obedience, for backsliding into sin. In this they are doubtless right—and I blame myself for the same thing; but I must at the same time bring them to see that that is our normal human condition. There is scarcely any such thing as a stable spiritual life. In any case it is rather a Hindu than a Christian ideal—the disappearance of the person, absorbed into the great Whole.

We do not 'possess' God, or contact with him. We find him periodically, and that is precisely the authentic and living religious experience. It is an adventure, of which the return of the Prodigal is an illustration, whereas the elder son, to whom the Father says 'Thou art ever with me' (Luke 15.31), undergoes no religious experience.

God has allowed man a greater margin of liberty than the animals. It is not only the organic margin of deviation of which we have spoken, and which by its fluctuations maintains the life of the body; it is a margin of moral disobedience which maintains, if I may put it so, his spiritual life. Viewed in this light, the moral conscience is seen to be exactly comparable with the organic sensitivity described by Dr Maurice Vernet. It is when we stray from the direction ordained by God, for his purpose, that it comes into action in order to bring us back. This coming back, which is repentance, reconciles us to God, and rekindles our spiritual life. To be more precise, it is not repentance which reconciles us to God, since this reconciliation comes to us from Jesus Christ by Grace; but repentance is the indispensable road that leads to it, as Christ himself said right at the beginning of his ministry: 'Repent: for the kingdom of heaven is at hand' (Matt. 4.17).

Thus God's plan for our spiritual life is realized, as in the life of the body, in a succession of corrections of our deviations. You remember what I said about the discordances between the person and the personage. The uneasiness to which they give rise, the overwhelming humiliation we feel when we recognize that we are not what we thought we were or wanted to be—those moments are so many decisive stages in our spiritual life: we are forced to our knees, and there find once more, through God's grace and forgiveness, harmony with him and with ourselves. We saw earlier that complete sincerity is an unattainable ideal. But what *is* attainable is the periodic movement of sincerity, the moment, in fact, when we confess that we are not as we have sought to appear; and it is at those moments that we find contact with God once more.

The progress of our spiritual life is made up of these successive discoveries, in which we perceive that we have turned away from God instead of going towards him. That is what makes a great saint like St Francis of Assisi declare himself chief among sinners. We cannot, indeed, be content with this fluctuating condition, any more than we can resign ourselves to always rediscovering discordances between our personage and our person. We hear Christ's command: 'Be ye therefore perfect, even as your Father which is in heaven is perfect' (Matt. 5.48). We find this intuitive aspiration towards perfection in unbelievers as well as in believers. It implies especially a complete concordance between personage and person. Now it is precisely because we feel the impossibility of following this call that we recognize our need of God and his grace, of Jesus Christ and his atonement. If we thought we did not need God, should we still have a spiritual life?

This spiritual life, in its characteristic sudden creative welling up, is therefore entirely subjective, inexpressible, and also intermittent. It is not manifested in the order of objectively observable phenomena except by its fruits: 'By their fruits ye shall know them' (Matt. 7.20). Now, these fruits are actually new automatisms, substituted for the old ones. St Paul enumerates them: 'The fruit of the Spirit is love, joy, peace, longsuffering, gentleness, goodness, faith, meekness, temperance' (Gal. 5.22-3).

To be sure, a fruit is a living thing. At the moment when the breath of the Spirit blows, all these qualities enumerated by the apostle well up like a spring of fresh water. But, inevitably, they gradually crystallize into new automatisms, and form a new personage. Thus piety is manifested in all the habits which go to make up this personage: regular prayer, confession, Bible-reading, the Church with all its rites and ceremonies. He who, on a plea of preserving spontaneity, refuses to submit to any religious discipline, will find his piety becoming extinguished. Just as we were unable to grasp life apart from the automatic living phenomena of the body and the mind, so we cannot conceive of spiritual life detached from all concrete and regular expression.

These automatisms are the necessary servants of the spiritual life whose support they are. The oft-repeated prayer, learnt in childhood, is a habit of the mind, an indispensable aid to the expression of our spiritual life. It is no more possible to detach such automatisms from the spiritual life they serve than to separate the personage from the person. Their repetition has stamped us with the ecclesiastical forms among which our religious life has developed, and to alter its rites is to endanger that life itself.

I remember a Roman Catholic who had divorced her husband.

She had remarried, and so had been excluded from communion in her Church. Her second husband was a Protestant, and she had willingly joined his Church, glad to be no longer excommunicate. Theological differences were a matter of no concern to her; on the contrary, she very sincerely adopted the dogmatic ideas of her new faith. But one day, when we had reached a stage of close personal contact, she suddenly asked me: 'Can you explain to me why it is that sometimes I can't pray?' And then she went on: 'I was accustomed to pray on my knees before holy images and candles, in an atmosphere of litanies. I feel numb in these Protestant churches; they are so bare.'

'There is nothing to stop you arranging a little oratory in your own room', I told her, 'with an image and a candle to kneel in front of.' My fellow Protestants will perhaps criticize me, but I record this because it seems to me that to help a soul to find God again is more important than any theological or ecclesiastical argument. It so happened that the next day another patient told me of how she had had the reverse experience. Hearing, in another Church than her own, the Lord's Prayer recited in quite a different tone of voice, she suddenly realized its riches and its meaning in a way she had not done for a very long time. Putting these two stories together, one sees clearly the double aspect of automatic actions: servants of life and obstacles to life.

Moreover, following up this line of thought, one can see that the force of habit constitutes a much greater obstacle to the reunion of the Christian Churches than doctrinal differences. Each Church cherishes its traditional forms, and all that I have written helps us to see that it is incapable of making any change in them unless a new creative explosion of spiritual life comes to overthrow these rigid automatisms.

This is clearly seen in the history of the Church.

From time to time God raises up saints or prophets—a St Francis of Assisi, a St Bernard, a Wesley. From their personal experience a renewal of life flows out, new forms of piety and obedience, a new language which helps those who were beginning to lose them to understand the eternal verities of the Gospel.

Little by little these forms and this language establish their own tradition, becoming sacrosanct formulae which will be broken down in their turn when there comes a new prophetic message. Thus, in the spiritual life too, automatisms, the necessary servants of life, are at the same time its tomb. These habits of piety, indispensable as I have shown them to be, can very quickly become emptied of their truly creative substance, to become nothing more than the cloak of a devout personage. There are bigoted stick-in-the-muds in every church. In a pious family it is easy to mistake for a living faith what is in reality only a system of rigid principles which imprison life.

In adolescence a child brought up in this sort of formalist environment may very well revolt against his parents and regard all their religious and moral traditions as a hollow farce or a strait-jacket. His indictment will have something in it of the accents of Christ himself when he inveighed against the Pharisees, those great religious personages of his day. They too were imprisoned within rigid principles whose distant source was in the revelation of the living God, though now there lingered only the automatisms it had left behind. Jesus Christ took his stand against them, saying: 'I am . . . the life' (John 11.25).

On the other hand, another child of that same family may possibly submit, and be stamped with the heavy imprint of its principles. He will be turned into a crushed and anguished being, with all his reactions determined for him. His parents, or perhaps his grandparents, have really had their lives shaken by the impact of the Spirit. But he himself has had no personal experience of it. The moral discipline which for the parents was quite spontaneous, is to him no more than an external constraint, a drill, a collection of automatisms.

Every psychotherapist has come across these tragic failures of moralism, a fact which has moved some theologians to join with certain psychotherapists in an attempt to restate the problem of asceticism in the light of the Bible and of modern psychology.[1] It is the impulse of the heart that has spiritual value, the willing

[1] *L'ascèse chrétienne et l'homme contemporain*, Editions du Cerf, Paris, 1951.

adoption of certain rules of life for the love of God—or, in psychological terms, what matters is the underlying 'motivation' of the adoption of such rules. Mortification motivated by a masochistic impulse cannot but be harmful.

Life, the Spirit, the person, are not substantial realities which we can hold in our hands. They cannot be docketed, analysed, or described. They are as fleeting as a lightning flash—by the time we have seen their light and heard the rumbling that follows them, they have already gone. We cannot reach the person either by means of introspection or by objective scientific study. Let us now, therefore, seek another way of approach.

PART THREE

THE PERSON

7

THE DIALOGUE

AFTER COMPLETING the previous chapter I left to take part in two medical conferences abroad. The second took place in Holland, a country which I have often visited already in order to attend similar meetings, promoted by my very dear friend Dr Jacob Ten Kate, now prematurely taken from us. A surgeon in the Hague, he had read my first book during the German occupation and had come to see me as soon as the liberation of his country made the journey possible. From then on he was, for me and my friends, a true comrade in arms in our efforts to give all human character back to modern medicine, which has become exclusively technical.

He had succeeded in gathering around himself an ever-widening circle of Dutch colleagues who shared his ideals. This year's meeting actually had as its theme the question: 'What is man?' There I heard, among other speeches, a remarkable address by Professor van den Berg of Utrecht, who, it is interesting to record, also spoke of the two possible methods of studying man which we have just been discussing: that of objective analysis, with its precise definitions and diagrams; and that, on the other hand, of introspection and living observation, which points to the ever changing diversity of human behaviour.

This contrast reminds us of the two kinds of spirit of which Pascal spoke, the spirit of geometry and the spirit of finesse. One relies on intelligence, the other on intuition; one is systematic, the other pragmatic; one seeks to demonstrate, the other only indicates; from one proceeds science, from the other, art. Which gives the truer picture? Are there not gaps in both?

Professor van den Berg soon showed us the insurmountable difficulties that have beset those who have chosen the road of analysis, of definitions and diagrams, ever since Descartes made his fundamental distinction between body and mind. Real life, real men, are not to be confined within any of the definitions we presume to make of them. There is no philosophical system or scientific knowledge that does not involve over-simplification. It is only by making an artificial intellectual abstraction that we can define such ideas as the mind, the body, or any of their elements; and since there is no living body without mind, or mind without body, men have been entangled for centuries in the insoluble problem of their relationship.

On the other hand, if one wishes only to depict man as he is, in all the richness of his being, one becomes lost in the inexhaustible variety of the aspects he presents, with their ever-changing nuances. More than that, the outlines of his person themselves become blurred. The speaker drew a comparison with a mountaineer, going over in his mind a projected climb, mentally picturing each movement he will make. The terrain has become as familiar to him as his own body, he identifies himself with it, becomes an integral part of it. We have already seen this in our description of the personage, those countless projections of ourselves upon everything around us, incorporating it into ourselves, into the picture we have of ourselves.

'Man is a world in himself!' Professor van den Berg concluded. He did not mean the microcosm of the old alchemists, in which they saw an order and a harmony that corresponded with those of the macrocosm, but rather a virgin forest of inextricably tangled growths without number or limit.

It is clear that while the first of these methods narrows man down to a mere abstraction, a diagram, a shell, convenient enough for study, but shorn of everything human and living, the other on the contrary enlarges and dilutes him to the point where his outlines disappear altogether. In the first method, the person is eclipsed behind the personage, a conventional image elaborated by the mind; in the second the person disappears behind a multitude of personages, behind all the many aspects presented successively or even simultaneously to the observer.

What the first method needs is a new dimension which would give man back his true nature; the second needs a guiding thread to help us to find our way through the virgin forest. It is in personal contact with other people that the answer to both these needs is to be found.

Indeed, what creates in me consciousness of self is the consciousness I have of a not-self, of an external world from which firstly I distinguish myself, which next I observe objectively from without, and with which I enter into relationship. Psychologists have described this birth of self-consciousness in the infant. There is, then, a double movement, first of separation and then of relation, between the self and things.

Next, what creates in me consciousness of being a person is entering into relationship with another person, the 'thou'. Here again we find the double movement: the consciousness of being distinct from another person, and the possibility of entering into personal relationship with him. The birth of the person may be illustrated from what happens in the case of secrets. Sir Edmund Gosse tells of an incident in his childhood through which he became aware of his own 'individuality'. It happened when at a certain point he realized that he knew something which his father did not know: 'The theory that my Father was omniscient or infallible was now dead and buried. . . . There was a secret in this world and it belonged to me.'[1]

The prestige of the secret is very great in the mind of the child, and this story shows us why. To know something which others do not, is to become a person, distinct from other persons. Thus, children like to invent secret codes which put a sort of barrier between them and their parents, and by means of which they are able to say things which the latter do not understand. Or else they make themselves secret hiding-places, and so are able to keep for themselves treasures to which their parents have no access.

A child's secrets must be respected. Something vitally important

[1] Sir Edmund Gosse, C.B., *Father and Son*, Evergreen Books, London, 1941, p. 34.

is at stake: nothing less than the formation of his person. Too often parents have no idea of the importance of these secrets. They think they have a right to know all about their child, even when he becomes adolescent—or even adult! This is denying his status as a person, it is keeping him in a childish state of dependence on his parents. On several occasions a mother has admitted to me that she has procured duplicate keys to her son's or her daughter's drawer in order to be able to go and see what they were hiding there, and to read their letters or private diaries.

I remember one of my patients, an orphan girl. She had an uncle who in her eyes was clothed with all the prestige of the scientist and philosopher. He used to carry out experiments in hypnosis on her. One day he had said to her: 'I know all your thoughts.' You can guess the effect of such an assertion—a veritable paralysing of the development of the person. To refuse a child the right to have a secret is to deny him that of becoming a person.

Often, for example, I have seen an only daughter, or one still living at home after all her brothers and sisters have married, who thought herself obliged to tell her mother everything, even at the age of thirty, forty or fifty. They always tell me that they would have a bad conscience about keeping anything from their mothers, as if it were wicked. The mothers consider it right and proper: 'I am my daughter's best friend', they will proudly tell me. They even encourage this false sense of guilt in the daughter: 'I met your friend Alice', they say, 'and she told me you'd been to see her,' adding reproachfully: 'You didn't tell me you had been.'

Such a daughter has as yet no experience of personal life. Her relationship with her mother is that of the child, not the adult. One has to be a person in order to establish personal contact with other people.

But while the child loves secrets, he also loves to tell them. 'I've got a secret', he says, 'but I'm not going to tell you it.' And then, a moment later: 'Don't you want me to tell you my secret?' And then, later still: 'I'd like to tell you my secret.' To enjoy having a secret and then to enjoy telling it is only apparently contradictory. In the first place, it is by telling it that one shows that there really was a secret. Many people, in this respect, remain children all their lives. They are incapable of resisting the pleasure of divulging secrets—they invent them if necessary—because of the prestige it procures them of knowing things of which everyone else is ignorant.

But there is a much deeper reason for the pleasure that the child has in telling his secret, and one which will reveal to us the first essential feature of the person: the free disposition of oneself. If I respect a child's secret, I am respecting his person, his autonomy as regards myself, his right to tell me what he likes and to hide from me what he likes, to dispose freely of himself. But when he surrenders his secret to me, it means that he has just as freely chosen me as his confidant, and by that free choice he is also affirming his status as a person, his right of self-determination.

Here again we have the double movement of which we were speaking just now: a separation followed by a relation. By the secret the person is formed, and then by communication of the secret it is affirmed. There was an infantile relationship when the daughter believed herself obliged to tell all her secrets to her mother. There is on the contrary a personal relationship when there is a free choice of a privileged confidant, the choice of a person by a person, a relationship between two persons—a dialogue.

The child who invents a secret code gives a friend the key to it: he can then say things to him that his parents do not understand. In this way he is manifesting the autonomy of his person. He did not choose his parents; his friend he *has* chosen, and introduced into intimacy with himself. In doing so he is acting as a person. He becomes a person through this contact with the 'thou'—through dialogue.

This is the situation obtaining in psychotherapy: to recount one's most private memories, the sort of thing one has never told anyone else, is to divulge one's secrets. In doing so my patient is revealing to me the things that are truly personal to him, things that I should be unable to guess from the appearances of him that I see, from the personage which he puts on in everyday life for the very purpose of hiding them.

This self-revelation has an astounding effect; this was Freud's first discovery. He at first attributed it to the fact that his patient was reliving in this way the harmful emotions of the past. This he called 'catharsis'. Soon he realized that it arose from a more important fact, the emotional relationship that was thus being established between his patient and himself, reproducing the attachment of the child to his father. This he named 'affective transference'.

Later, Dr Maeder showed[1] that something quite different again was involved: not merely an emotional bond—a psychological phenomenon—but a 'personal contact', a true spiritual event. The psychotherapist differs from the father in that he is freely chosen. The confidence shown in him by his patient is thus more than a mark of infantile affection; it is an act of adulthood, of self-determination, a personal commitment in a dialogue between persons.

We have returned once more to the distinction pointed out in the preceding chapter between a psychological phenomenon and a spiritual event. Although personal contact is established through the body or the mind, through touch or affection, it is essentially a spiritual fact, inasmuch as it is specifically human.

When I was a child, submerged in my 'orphan complex', I was very reserved with my comrades; I preferred the companionship of my dog, and spent much of my time with him; it was to him that I told my secrets, just as a little girl tells hers to a doll. By telling my secrets to an animal, I avoided the risk both of having them given away and of being criticized. The element of choice was there, but there was no dialogue. We have come to the second fundamental characteristic of the person: responsibility. True personal relationship, of the sort that makes the person,

[1] A. Maeder, *La personne du médecin, un agent psychothérapeutique.*

involves both, choice and risk it lays one open to a reply, and to the necessity of replying in turn: it is a dialogue.

This, then, is the meaning of Dr Aloys von Orelli's formula: 'The person, a dialogue.'[1] Man shares with the animals the functions of the body and the mind, touch and affection. But man alone can enter into a responsible dialogue, maintain his personal convictions, at the risk of being judged or betrayed. 'Man is person inasmuch as he can speak, and inasmuch as one can speak to him and with him,' writes Professor Seifert.[2]

About 1920 Martin Buber published a book entitled *I and Thou*,[3] which aroused considerable interest. It was as if man's spiritual communion with others, which is peculiar to him, had been rediscovered after centuries of individualism. The whole difference between an individual and a person is that the individual associates, whereas the person communicates. There is the same difference between the personage and the person; the personage is an external appearance which touches the personage of others from outside, the person communicates inwardly with the second person, the 'thou'.

This is the new dimension which eludes the objective scientific study of man. Science, in order to study man, takes him in himself, as an individual and not as a person, isolating him from his environment; it is able to analyse his physical and psychical relationships with his environment, but it cannot have any knowledge of his spiritual relationship, his personal communion with his fellows.

This personal relationship is also the guiding thread we were seeking. In the thick and limitless forest of our life, in the tangle of experiences, impressions, attitudes and appearances, so many that one could never enumerate them all, everything is not of equal value.

In the life of each of us there are decisive hours that tell us

[1] Aloys von Orelli, *Persönlichkeit, Selbst, Person*, Georg Thieme, Stuttgart, 1951.

[2] Quoted by A. Maeder, *Le rôle du contact affectif en psychothérapie.*

[3] English translation by Ronald Gregor Smith, T. & T. Clark, Edinburgh, 1937.

more about the person than all the rest of our lives put together.
Do I say hours? Minutes, seconds, rather; moments which are to
determine the whole course of our lives thereafter. Remember
the motorist, in Chapter 5, and how we contrasted his considered
and isolated turning of the steering-wheel at the cross-roads in
order to take the chosen direction, with the innumerable and
imperceptible automatic corrections he applies through the
steering-wheel in order to keep himself going in the direction
he has thus taken.

Now, the cross-roads is this moment of true dialogue, of
personal encounter with another person, which obliges us to
take up a position with regard to him, to commit ourselves.
Even to run away is to make some sort of decision, choosing a
side-road in order to evade the dialogue. Most of the incessant
fluctuations of our being and of our behaviour, actions and words
are, as in the animals, merely reflex responses to an external
stimulus, manifestations of the personage. At the moment of
true dialogue, of inner personal communion, we cannot avoid
taking up a position, and in this genuine responsible act the
person is unveiled. That is why Sartre writes: 'I cannot know
myself except through the intermediary of another person.'[1]
It is symptomatic, in this connection, that when we hear a
recording of our own voice we do not recognize it.

Of course I am here making a distinction, in order to measure
their significance, between two dialogues which always go
together. We have already seen that the person pure and simple
does not exist. The real inner encounter, the true dialogue which
commits us, is enveloped in the external dialogue which expresses
it. Even when this communication is felt in silence, which we are
fond of saying is more eloquent than speech, this silence is itself
charged with the words that have been exchanged before it began.[2]

I was thinking about this the other day, at the end of a lengthy
conversation which had ended in deep silence. And my patient
noticed it at the same time as I did: we felt that there had been

[1] Jean-Paul Sartre, *L'être et le néant*, N. R. F., Paris, 1943.
[2] See Georges Gusdorf, *La parole*.

going on between us a double dialogue; one apparent and visible, formed of our words, our confidences, our looks and our gestures —an encounter of personages; the other inward and invisible— the encounter of our persons. The second could not have existed without the first, but the first had no value except as an expression of the second.

If then there is, as one of my friends writes to me, only one language, that of our words, gestures and signs, in fact of the whole movement of our being, that language has two meanings: one nourishes and satisfies the personage, while the other, more 'intrinsic', always immanent, is always expressed and perceived by the person. And there, my friend adds, is the element of security which permits us to believe in the person in spite of the evidence of the personage; the key-element which makes dialogue always possible.

In the multitudinous contacts of social life, however, how often do we thus commit our inmost selves in the apparent dialogue? One can chat endlessly, engage in abstruse intellectual arguments, read whole libraries and so make the acquaintance of all kinds of authors, travel the world over, be a dilettante collector of all sorts of impressions, react like an automaton to every caprice of sentiment, without ever really encountering another person, or discovering oneself by taking up a position with regard to him. Think of the haste and superficiality of modern life, radio programmes flitting from one triviality to another, the 'permanent' cinema, 'Digests' that skim over everything, organized touring that leaves no time for really making contact with things and people.

I was thinking recently of the true meaning of travel, in the incomparable setting of the island of Mikonos, one of the Cyclades. Before the meeting in Holland of which I have spoken, we had been in Greece where the 'Medicine of the Person Week' was being held that year. I was preparing for it, and contemplating the town, set like a brilliant dash of white between the blue of the sea and the blue of the sky, with, in the distance, the islet of Delos, which, so the legend has it, Zeus caused to rise from the waters to provide a birth-place for Apollo.

The real meaning of travel, like that of a conversation by the fireside, is the discovery of oneself through contact with other people, and its condition is self-commitment in that dialogue. Those old Greek gods are not just poetry and legend. In them the Ancients personified living realities—intelligence, beauty, love or lust, which are still at work in our hearts, and which fashion our person. The language they speak is that of image and myth, which touches the person much more directly than the explicit language of science and the intellectual dialectic of the modern world.

It is also the language of the Bible, of the parables of Christ, which the rationalist of today finds it so difficult to understand, of the Word of God which demands of us not a discussion but a personal decision. Again, it is the language of the human heart, when it casts off the intellectualism in which it has been trained at school, and recovers its pristine freshness. It is the language of our dreams. A thing that strikes me when I am talking with my patients is that the moment deep personal contact is made, the very style of our talk changes. Images spring spontaneously to the mind, we begin to talk in parables, and we understand one another better than when the tone of our conversation was intellectual and didactic. The conversation becomes anecdotal, as the Bible is anecdotal, as the *Iliad* and the *Odyssey* are anecdotal; but the anecdote is no longer then merely a story, it is an experience, a personal truth.

And then for us doctors Greece meant Hippocrates and Epidaurus. It meant those origins of our art in which men understood much better than they do today the nature of the human person; a medicine which, in Hippocrates, understood man in his unity and in his relationship with his environment, and which at Epidaurus succeeded in combining the physical treatment of the body with a real psychotherapy and with spiritual influence.[1]

[1] See F. Trensz, 'Die Entwicklung der Medizin und die Aufgaben der "Medizin der Person"', *Wege zum Menschen*, Vandenhoeck & Ruprecht, Göttingen, 1954, Heft 8.

Classical Greece was a civilization of the person.[1] Consider their schools, with their real personal contact between the master and his disciples, their community life. Myths and poetry, music and the stadium all contributed to a formation of the person that was much deeper and more harmonious than is the case with our modern schools with their arid accumulation of intellectual information.

Finally consider Plato, the dialogues, Socrates, bringing those with whom he talked face to face with the lucid discovery of themselves, and committing his own person so completely in his convictions that he was able to undergo the test of martyrdom. He likens himself to his mother, the midwife: he is the midwife of the person. He pitilessly unmasks the sophisms of the personage, the fine theories that have no genuine roots.

And then we opened our Bibles in Corinth, on the spot where St Paul appeared before Gallio and engaged with him in the true dialogue reported in Chapter 18 of the Acts of the Apostles. Greece is the place where the Gospel first took root in the Europe whose history it was to mould. And the instrument was the Apostle Paul, a man so personal that in him doctrine and experience are one, who speaks to the multitude solely in order to touch men personally and to compel them to make a choice, just as he himself was constrained by Jesus Christ to total commitment.

It was not only memories of the past that we met in Greece. We met men too, men that were very much alive, like the militant Christians of the Christian Union of Intellectuals, of the *ZΩH* community, of the Hellenikon Phos, who are leading their country towards a great spiritual revival, and who have sketched, in *Towards a Christian Civilization*[2] the outline of a civilization of the person. We were given the opportunity of renewing the fruitful dialogue between Christians of East and West, almost completely suspended by the Great Schism.

How many really personal encounters are there, with the

[1] See A. N. Tsirintanes, 'Griechische Kultur, Christlicher Glaube und Menschliche Person', *Wege zum Menschen*, 1954, Heft 7.

[2] Published (in English) in Athens, 1948.

barriers of the personage down between Christians of the various confessions? And yet the fact is that we need them, in order to discover our own persons and to discover each other; in order to see ourselves as we are, and not according to the picture we have had of ourselves, distorted by prejudice; in order to find once more, beneath the superficial differences, the intimate communion of person with person.

How are we to establish this true dialogue which we now see as the means of access to the person? Is it a matter of natural sympathy? If so it would be singularly restricted; it would be made dependent upon a simple affective function, upon an automatism. That would be to turn things the wrong way round —indeed, even the passion of love itself is powerless to establish it between a man and wife when each is keeping himself to himself.

On the contrary, when contact takes place between two persons, the antipathy or indifference which has kept them apart vanishes. One of my friends once remarked: 'I used to be able to put my patients into two categories, the congenial and the uncongenial. But now that I have begun to get interested in them as persons, I find them all congenial.'

Is it a matter of temperament? There are of course people who talk much more than others. There are even those who are very ready to talk about themselves. But one can talk a great deal, even about oneself—too much, perhaps—and yet say nothing really personal, nothing that is likely to lead to personal contact. And the opposite is true: there are some psychoanalysts, who follow the Freudian rule of silence, who can undoubtedly establish personal contact with their patients.

Others have actually substituted the dialogue for the Freudian monologue, and Dr Maeder has stressed the vital significance of this change of method.[1] But when he describes what takes place in psychotherapy as a 'relationship in dialogue', I take him to mean, not so much the external form of the dialogue, as the

[1] *La personne du médecin, un agent psychothérapeutique.*

spirit animating both patient and doctor, their mutual attitude on a deeper level.

Personally, I am a very silent man. Some of my patients criticize me on that score. But that complaint does not come from those with whom I am able to make the closest contact, for they are well aware that personal commitment is not to be measured by the number of words that one utters.

Perhaps it is something my patient confides in me that all at once awakens personal memories. That problem that he reveals has troubled me a great deal. It still worries me. That temptation he tells me of, I know it too. That lapse he confesses, I have been guilty of similar ones. That disagreement he has had with his wife. I have had the very same one with mine.

'Why do you smile like that?' he asks me suddenly.

'I was just realizing that you aren't so very different from me as you think.'

And I begin to tell him of my own personal experiences. I try to be as honest with that man as he is with me. The result is that the picture he had of me, as a personage wearing a halo of science, of faith, and of moral perfection—a role which, in spite of all my concern for honesty, I was not entirely innocent of playing in front of him—vanishes, allowing him a glimpse of my true person. We have both of us left convention behind, we are really encountering each other. This was what Dr Dubois of Berne, one of the pioneers of modern psychotherapy, meant when he said as far back as 1905: 'Hold out your hand then to that poor sick man. Do not be afraid of frankly admitting to him your weaknesses, your inborn shortcomings. Bring yourself close to him.'[1]

This change of tone marks the beginning of a true dialogue, for then the personage effaces itself, and allows the person to appear. It depends sometimes on the briefest word, provided it be really personal, or even on quite intangible factors. It is not peculiar to the psychotherapy of the sick; it can be felt at any moment of our everyday life. Those who helped me most to free

[1] *Les psychonévroses et leur traitement morale*, Masson, Paris, 1905.

myself from the complex I had as the result of being an orphan, which kept me reserved and unsociable until after the age of thirty, and which blocked for me the road to personal contact, were not doctors, much less specialists. They were my wife and those of my friends who, because they were themselves no longer slaves of the personage, were frank and open with me.

In my turn I saw that by adopting a more personal tone myself I was helping others to become personal, not only in my consulting-room, but in the most ordinary conversation in the street, on military service, or in a medical conference. And I realized how men thirst for this real contact, from which new life springs up to blow like a fresh breeze among us and within us.

Then a man is enabled, almost without noticing it, to tell me about things that have been lying heavy on his heart perhaps for years. Suddenly he breaks off, as if astonished at himself: "I don't know why I tell you all this; I've never told anyone else. I never thought I should be able to tell anyone.' And he adds, looking me in the eyes: 'What a relief it is to get it all off one's chest!'

This quality of the dialogue has often been given the name of 'transparency'. It is a beautiful image, but nevertheless I must be honest here too, as I write this book. Let us admit at once that complete transparency is a utopian ideal, just as we have previously recognized as utopian the hope of seeing the person shorn competely of its personage.

As a friend of mine remarked in a letter recently, the person is a whole vast domain, a country. We enter it, constantly dis-discovering new prospects as we go. But it is too vast and complex, too restlessly alive for us ever to know and comprehend it fully.

It is the sudden flash of honesty, the moment of transparency, which overwhelms us and transfigures the climate of our relationships with other people. There is no such thing as complete transparency. There is only one supremely privileged relationship in which we approach anywhere near it, and that is marriage.

That is what imparts to marriage, when it is a true dialogue, its incomparable richness, its prodigious capacity for developing the person and showing us ourselves as we really are.

From even before the time they are formally engaged, there are two roads open to a man and a woman who love each other: that which leads to transparency and that of the calculated effect, that of the person or that of the formation of a personage. One always feels, in the first flush of love, that transparency will be easy. 'I can tell my fiancé everything, because I feel he understands me.'

But the true dialogue has hardly begun yet. The true dialogue is not that first easy communion, wonderful though it be—the impression one has of sharing the same feelings, saying the same things and thinking the same thoughts. The true dialogue is inevitably the confrontation of two personalities, differing in their past, their upbringing, their view of life, their prejudices, their idiosyncrasies and failings—and in any case with two distinct psychologies, a man's and a woman's. Sooner or later they will find out that they are less alike than they thought.

Either, one will dominate the other, and there will no longer be a dialogue because one of the persons is eclipsed, his power of self-determination paralysed. Or else the course of the dialogue will take it through some very dangerous waters. One of the partners will find himself saying to the other: 'I can't understand why you are acting like this.' And then there arises the risk of being judged or betrayed, of which we have spoken, and the temptation to run away from it by keeping back certain confidences.

In many homes it is actually, by a strange paradox, concern for marital harmony and the desire to safeguard love, which gradually turns the partners away from transparency: 'I don't talk about that subject with my husband; it irritates him. He gets annoyed at once, and we quarrel, and both let ourselves be carried away into saying things we regret. What's the good? All it does is to put us a little further apart.'

Do not misunderstand me: I am not criticizing that attitude.

Occasionally it is the least bad solution. Through it, in a large number of homes, a married couple is able to preserve a certain apparent harmony. They may still know some fine moments, and share many joys and sorrows, but they become more and more strangers one to another. Real dialogue becomes more and more difficult between them.

It is always a denial of love, and to some extent a disavowal of marriage, to begin to calculate what one says and does not say, even when it is done with the excellent motive of safeguarding one's love. It is a contradiction of the law of marriage instituted by God: 'They are no more twain, but one flesh' (Matt. 19.6). There is no question here, as there is in the child's relationship with his parents, of a right to keep secrets, since the marriage partner has actually been chosen freely as a privileged confidant. The same biblical text expressly says: 'For this cause shall a man leave father and mother, and shall cleave to his wife' (Matt. 19.5, Gen. 2.24).

But even in the happiest marriage personal contact cannot be a permanent state, acquired once and for all. The windows of our houses have to be cleaned from time to time if the light is to penetrate. They get dirty more quickly in the town, but there is no countryside so remote or so clean that they do not gradually lose their transparency. Between man and wife too, the true dialogue has periodically to be re-established by the confession of some secret; and the higher and more sincere our ideal of marriage, the more irksome it is to admit that we have hidden something.

What we said about secrets is true in the domain of sex: there is a double movement, first of retreat and then of self-abandonment. The true meaning of modesty is to be found in this retention of a secret which will one day be handed over to the person of our choice, with whom it will thereafter constitute an unbreakable bond, a commitment. Without perhaps knowing anything yet of the distant goal of her instinct, a young girl begins to feel reluctant to undress in front of her parents. The latter sometimes think that this modesty in regard to them is silly. They are making the same mistake, and doing the same damage to their daughter, as in violating a secret.

The appearance of this sense of shame is, in fact, the sign of the birth of the person. And later the supreme affirmation of the person, the great engagement of life, self-determination, will be marked by the handing over of the secret, the gift of the self, the disappearance of shame.

But there are many married people, the victims of false suggestions or of psychological disturbances, who do not fully experience this reversal. Caring passionately for spiritual communion or moral candour, they still feel embarrassed by physical contact, without realizing that that is just as great a denial of the true dialogue of marriage.

There are others, however, who somehow seek, in the strong feeling of unity which the sexual bond gives, to shirk the moral dialogue. They evade the difficult encounter of personalities which we decribed, by taking the easy road of physical love. This can be seen even from the time of the engagement: those who anticipate matters and give themselves to each other before marriage are always to some extent deceiving themselves. They think they are giving a sign of the 'engagement' of their hearts, when in fact they are weakening its significance, since full responsibility is not assumed in a clandestine relationship, but only in the 'I will' of marriage in Church or the signature in the registry office.

With even greater reason, of course, sexual intercourse outside marriage and the promise of marriage is a sort of abdication of the person, since it takes place without any constraint of responsibility.

Marriage thus becomes a great school of the person, through the level of personal commitment it entails and the exacting quality of the dialogue it demands.

The difficulty of the celibate life does not arise only from the temptations caused by the unfulfilment of instinctive urges, but also from the fact that the true dialogue with the other sex awakens precisely this danger of the introduction of secret overtones and undertones of sexual love. But the celibate's safeguard against this danger is again a commitment of himself, one that is quite as exacting as that of marriage, namely his commitment of himself to God, which imposes on him a strict moral vigilance. This, for the celibate, is the price of his entry into that dialogue with the opposite sex which is so enriching to the person.

8

THE OBSTACLE

HERE I AM on the threshold of a new chapter. At the end of the preceding one my thoughts were flowing easily, and I seemed to have no difficulty in putting them into words. Now I sit in front of a blank sheet of paper, my brain in a whirl as I try to formulate the subject-matter of this chapter. I waste time; I shuffle the little pieces of paper on which I have jotted down my ideas, not knowing where to begin. A feeling of fatigue invades me.

I know very well what is happening. The same thing occurs in the course of an interview. Personal contact is ever a fragile thing, unstable and insecure. It has to be found again at each meeting. When it is established words come easily, and seem all true, all to have life and substance. But beforehand they seemed hollow, conventional, trivial. We are somehow embarrassed as we approach one another. Lack of contact causes embarrassment and embarrassment makes contact more difficult. My patient and I are both seeking contact, and in order to find it we hide our embarrassment under a cloak of banalities, witticisms and digressions. Each feels that the other knows very well what we are doing, and that makes our embarrassment worse.

To write is also to establish a dialogue with my reader, a dialogue whose replies I imagine. I have formulated in my mind the first sentence of this chapter: 'If there is in all of us such a thirst for this true dialogue, why then is it so rare and so difficult to establish?' At once I picture the critical reactions of my readers. For one, I am splitting hairs, making everything far too complicated; I am being morbid; personal contact is not so rare in healthy people; it is enough to be simple and open-hearted, without losing oneself in all this subtle analysis. Another will think my sentence nothing but a glimpse of the obvious: is it really necessary to write books in order to express what everybody knows all the time? It is like using a battering-ram on an open door.

A third will consider that I am abusing the expression 'true dialogue', or will complain of my style. No one doubts that I am trying to write as well as I can, and attempting to make an original contribution to the study of the human person. If, therefore, I do not write better, it is because I am incapable of doing so. I am to be judged all the more severely in that I am going to send what I write to the printers. Perhaps, indeed, one ought to heed the words of the fabulist: 'In order to live happy, live hidden.'

And so one hides; or rather, one is divided between showing oneself and hiding. Suppose someone has just paid me a compliment. Instead of telling him that what he says pleases me enormously, I pass it off with a hollow protest. But of course this affectation of modesty does not deceive him. I am reminded of a remark made by one of my patients: 'Life is a universal game of hide-and-seek in which we just pretend to hide.' And yet I do desire this personal contact. It is even a thing that I am particularly greedy for; it is one of the things that I value most in life.

Here too I should like to have direct contact with my reader, to talk to him without beating about the bush, to let him share in these thoughts that have long haunted my mind, and which perhaps occupy his mind too, to tell him my beliefs. Now that I have confessed to him what it was that was holding me back— this foolish fear of his criticisms—I already feel easier about doing it. I am less afraid that he will reproach me for talking too much about myself. What I want, in fact, is to put into a book not only my ideas, but my person.

Thus the obstacle to contact is not only in the external circumstances of the modern world which we have described; nor is it only in our uncertainty about what we really are. It is much bigger. It is a positive force, an instinct that prompts us to run away in order to avoid the dialogue. As my friend Jean de Rougemont has remarked, 'man seeks man and flees from him'.[1]

[1] *Op. cit.*

Think of what goes to make up most conversations: the exchange of superficial impressions ('What gorgeous weather!'); conventional remarks that do not always come from the heart ('How are you?'); observations whose true intention is self-justification or more or less cleverly to make the most of oneself; flattery; straight-forward or veiled criticism. Here again I must beware of utopianism: it would simply not be human to wish to divest the dialogue of everything superfluous; it would become dry and pedantic, devoid of all graciousness and poetry.

The small-talk of everyday life can be a genuine road towards contact, a way of getting to know somebody, a prelude to more profound exchanges, a simple and natural approach. But, let us admit it, it is also often used as a means of avoiding personal contact. It is like a prologue that goes on so long that the play never begins. It allows us to be friendly and interesting with people without touching on subjects that would compel us to enter into real dialogue.

Each of us does his best to hide behind a shield. For one it is a mysterious silence which constitutes an impenetrable retreat. For another it is facile chit-chat, so that we never seem to get near him. Or else it is erudition, quotations, abstractions, theories, academic argument, technical jargon; or ready-made answers, trivialities, or sententious and patronizing advice.

One hides behind his timidity, so that we cannot find anything to say to him; another behind a fine self-assurance which renders him less vulnerable. At one moment we have recourse to our intelligence, to help us to juggle with words. Later on we pretend to be stupid so that we can reply as if we had not understood. It is possible to hide behind one's advanced years, or behind one's university degree, one's political office, or the necessity of nursing one's reputation. A woman can hide behind her startling beauty, or behind her husband's notoriety; just as, indeed, a husband can hide behind his wife. The personage is the willing watch-dog of the person.

A joke or a witty remark is always an easy way of breaking off an embarrassing dialogue. I am not here condemning wit, which is one of the graces of life. When I take up an illustrated journal the first thing I look at is the humorous cartoons. The vocation of the humorist seems to me to be eminently beneficent: he is able to get some valuable truth across much more directly and more delicately than the moralist. Doubtless we more often look at his work in order to laugh at others than to examine ourselves. But I am exposed to the same sort of abuse as are the humorists: I remember a lady once saying to me triumphantly: 'I made my husband read such and such a passage in your book— what you said exactly applies to him.' I need scarcely mention that personal contact between those two had not been thereby improved!

When the dialogue is becoming too embarrassing all that is necessary is to make a passing allusion to some current controversial topic, to politics, or to some much-discussed artist. The conversation is immediately side-tracked on to an inoffensive subject, or at least one that is much more impersonal—perhaps one that provides an opportunity for a display of erudition or of unusual opinions.

Work, too, can be used as a defensive shield. There are men who bring work home every evening so as to have an excuse for not entering into any serious conversation with their wives or children. Others barricade themselves behind the newspaper as soon as they get home, pretending to be deeply absorbed in it when their wives try to tell them of their troubles. Others put on the wireless. They have a concert to listen to or a match to follow just at the one moment when there might be a possibility of calmly discussing important and pressing decisions that have to be taken. A woman brings her son to see me. His future is in jeopardy on account of serious moral troubles; he has just been sent down from his university. 'And what does your husband think about all this?' I ask. 'Oh, my husband! As soon as I try to talk to him seriously about anything he picks up his hat and goes off to his club!'

Often, without realizing it, a woman takes refuge from the dialogue in her domestic chores: she always has to do some ironing that cannot wait, or else she has to see that the children get on with their homework. By what amounts to a secret understanding many couples constantly avoid being alone together. They are always having visitors, or going to see a show. For their holidays they go off with a troop of friends.

It is a truism that a dialogue can only take place between two people. As soon as a third is added, however close and intimate he be, the tone of the conversation becomes less personal. I see this clearly enough when a patient comes to an interview in company with some relative. Even if it is a man who brings his wife who already knows all that he is going to say to me, he says it partly for her benefit, and not solely for mine. The moment there is a gallery we cannot help playing to it a little.

'I am coming to pay you a flying visit . . .' can mean 'I am not disposed to broach with you the question which we are both thinking about, and which really calls for a frank explanation.' Even without saying anything, but by using gestures suggestive of haste, one can give one's partner to understand that he must not draw one into a difficult or serious discussion. There are many people like that, always in a hurry, never allowing themselves to be tied down. They rush from one activity to another, with magnificent devotion and tremendous zeal. So long as they are concerning themselves with technical problems, they are prepared to exercise a lively intelligence and all their ability. But they have no time to spare for the more intimate remarks which alone create a personal bond.

They often themselves deplore the fact. But so far from lightening their programme, they add to it; and when they are tired, their very tiredness can be used as a screen. A businessman comes home late, worn out, and his wife understands that he does not wish to be bothered with domestic problems—he is already over-burdened with responsibilities outside. But it happens too that a wife holds the children back whenever they try to make contact with their father: 'Daddy is very tired; we must leave him in peace.'

The fact that an illness or an infirmity shuts one off from life is always for the person concerned an added suffering. But it is also, often without his realizing it, a protection against the hurly-burly of life. It is possible then for an unconscious fear of healing to insinuate itself into the mind; for recovery would oblige the sufferer once more to face problems from which his sickness spares him. Thus there may be set up within him an obstacle to healing.

Or else a very real and very painful migraine, a distressing liver attack, or a stubborn diarrhoea may manifest themselves every time one has to deal with a difficult situation. People who are hard of hearing have confessed to me, too, that they have sometimes been grateful to their infirmity for allowing them to evade an unwelcome dialogue. The same is true of nervousness, sensitiveness or bad temper, which are often like a warning notice: 'Do not touch'. Good humour, of course, or an air of unassailable sprightliness, can equally act as a screen.

It is the same with the phenomenon which modern psychology calls 'infantile regression'. It often happens that adults who are well-developed in other respects (in their intellectual or professional life, for example) behave like children in certain circumstances—in their relationship with their wives, from whom they expect the sort of protection a mother affords; with their fathers, whom they are still afraid to oppose; or with a friend, whom they invest with the magical prestige of a hero. To become adult would in fact mean to enter into certain dialogues as equals, and they evade them by means of infantile reactions.

I was thinking of this only today, talking to a business-man. It was his wife who had come to see me first. But after each of our conversations she used to discuss with her husband all she had discovered about herself. It is a lovely thing to have a husband and wife thus developing together and having the feeling of falling in love again. That is what marriage really means: helping one another to reach the full status of being persons, responsible and autonomous beings who do not run away from life.

Today it was the husband who came to see me and to tell me of his new experiences. He added frankly: 'It makes life fascinating, but it isn't easy, when one has decided not to run away from it any longer!'

'That's true, isn't it?' I answered. 'We are always looking for protection, building little shelters against the storms of life.'

Money, reputation and work can thus be used as refuges. Money, through the air of importance it confers; through the gratitude aroused by the munificence it enables us to practise. One has seen parents effectively silence their children by giving them bank-notes; even when the children are grown up and married, they keep their relationship with them on an infantile level, preventing them from treating them as equals, by keeping them in a state of financial dependence under colour of generosity. One has seen husbands who put their wives off with a present, when what is really required is an explanation.

I recall once realizing, in giving to a patient one of those samples of medicines that doctors are always getting in abundance, that what I was really doing was saving myself the trouble of a serious talk. It would have been long and difficult, and I happened to be in a hurry. I remember the case very well: at the end of her consultation a woman suddenly said to me: 'I don't know what to do for my husband. He is never free of colds—none of the specialists have been able to do anything for him.' In a flash, my own experience came into my mind. I too had once been subject to colds for months on end. I had found it necessary to reorganize my life completely in order to raise the level of my physical resistance. But how could I explain all that in a few minutes? It is so far removed from the usual over-simple and mechanistic idea of disease. So I took from my cupboard a preparation of antiseptic oil, saying: 'Tell him to try this.'

If we have rendered a service to somebody, even when it has cost us nothing, we feel that we have no need to do anything about the more personal aid that we ought to have given him. That is true over the whole field of professional life: to do one's duty, fulfil one's technical function, give the client what he has a right as a client to expect—to do all this is to feel oneself discharged from the obligation of adding to it what he might expect as a human being.

The technical function is essentially impersonal. In order to make his diagnosis the doctor coldly puts his precise questions. He goes through the necessary motions and manipulates the necessary instruments. He pursues within himself a scientific debate in which the point at issue is of considerable importance. The whole process creates an atmosphere of detachment which often makes it difficult to enter into a more personal dialogue. But at times he knows in his heart of hearts that he ought to do so; he knows too that it is more difficult than all this technical activity which permits him to evade it. He is doing his job as a doctor, which is an immense enough task in all conscience. One cannot complain if he confines himself strictly to that.

The same is true of all professions. What M. Jules Romains calls the 'Official System',[1] the game at which the whole of society is adept, in which each member punctiliously fulfils the duty imposed upon him by convention, is no longer seen only as an annoying obstacle in the way of personal contact, but rather as a grille behind which we shelter our fragile person.

We conceal our person behind a protective barrier; we let it be seen only through the bars. We display certain of its aspects, others we carefully hide. It is not, as one might suppose, that we are careful only of our weaknesses, but sometimes of our most precious possessions. How many people are there who secretly write poems, which they carefully lock away, or who turn some inaccessible attic corner into an artist's studio.

There comes to see me a mystic, who on several occasions has had visions. I am enthralled by what he tells me. I discover that this apparently rational man has a profound intuition regarding spiritual matters, amounting to veritable revelations. Only once, he tells me, did he broach the subject with his brother, not openly, but by a discreet allusion; and he felt, or thought he felt, that his brother was beginning to wonder if he was quite sane. Since

[1] Jules Romains, *Les hommes de bonne volonté*, VI: *Les humbles*, Flammarion, Paris.

then he has carefully kept his treasure to himself. Now I understand why he asked me a moment ago what difference there was between visions and hallucinations.

The more costly an experience is to us, the greater its significance in our lives and the more it occupies our minds—and also the more are we afraid of its being misunderstood, or that it will be cheapened by some misapplied remark or suspicion. The more refined and subtle our minds, the more vulnerable they are. When we are alone we are haunted by doubts about the genuineness of our deepest intuitions and feelings—like my friend the mystic. What hurts him in fact is the contrast between his life as seen by others, and his secret life which is entirely dominated by the visions he has had.

Thus, although we are made to suffer by reason of the discordance between our personage and our person, of which I have spoken, nevertheless we carefully foster it for fear of having our person hurt if we reveal its most precious treasures. This is often what happens in the case of our artistic, philosophical or religious convictions. We feel they are still too fragile to stand up to being judged and even brutally contradicted by others. But our convictions are never really clear and firm until they have been expressed and defended.

We guard our treasures, and that treasure of treasures, our person. Yesterday one of my patients said to me: 'I think that what I have really been doing is to spend my life defending myself against everybody.' It is true that people are quick to pass judgment; they break the beginner's spirit by pointing out his smallest blunders; they maintain their own self-confidence by decrying those who have real talent. One cannot escape from the jealousy which is so quick to criticize. Let us admit that we are afraid and that we go on hiding our fears. 'The art of living', writes Dr Forel,[1] 'is the art of concealing one's own original fear, while at the same time exploiting the fears of others.'

But of course what we are most afraid of is exposing to view

[1] Oscar Forel, 'Peur, panique et politique', in *Revue suisse de psychologie*, 1942, Nos. 1 and 2.

our faults and shortcomings. Many people deny that man is as I describe him. 'To read your books', they tell me, 'one would think that there were tragedies in every family, skeletons in every cupboard! You are the victim of a sort of occupational disease that has warped your perception.' Others put it down to my Calvinist pessimism.[1] But it seems to me that in fact their optimism is to some extent due to their naïvety. They let themselves be deceived by appearances.

I do not see the sick only, but a good number of the healthy as well. Their resolve to be more candid and open in my consulting-room than they ordinarily are permits me to see what is going on behind the façade of their lives. There are extremely respectable families—families that my critics would readily quote as examples —in which scarcely a meal passes without some violent scene taking place, and even blows being exchanged. Refined and intelligent personalities, nothing of this could be suspected from their distinguished and courteous behaviour in front of even the least important of guests.

It is precisely when they have the highest ideals, when they are most cultured, educated and refined, that men are most ashamed of their secret behaviour in certain circumstances, and that they do everything to hide it. It is precisely because they do not understand why they do not manage to exercise self-control that they judge themselves severely, and then are afraid of being similarly judged by others. Rough, uncultured people are much more willing to show themselves in their true colours.

Look at the resistance put up by some families to the suggestion by one of their members that he should consult a psychologist. They fear that he will betray family secrets; they pester him, trying to find out what he has said about his private life; they resort to violent accusations and threats. Or it may be, on the contrary, that a man's family life is beautiful and serene, while he carefully hides what is going on in his professional life. If there is not a tragedy in every life, at any rate in every home

[1] P. W. E. Bibliographical note in *For Health and Healing*, London, March, 1954.

there are plenty of unpleasant things that could be told. This is what Bergson means when he speaks somewhere of a secret universally kept: a secret which we respect in others so that they will respect ours.

I am not, of course, thinking only of major tragedies. In the minor details of life we find it just as irksome that people should see all sorts of little facets of ourselves which do not fit in with the picture of ourselves that we wish others to have. Again and again we are perfectly well aware that the real motive of our attitude is simply idleness, self-conceit, jealousy, self-interest, covetousness or ambition. We cover it up quickly under some flattering explanation. We are faced with a difficult case, and launch out into a lengthy dissertation, full of scientific jargon, in order to conceal our ignorance. Have I forgotten a patient's name? While I am hunting for it in my memory I pay him somewhat exaggerated attention; or else I make allusion to minor points in our previous interviews to show him that I remember them. Have I forgotten a letter which I promised to write? I excuse myself by stressing how busy I am.

I remember one day at the end of a long walk with a colleague, during which we had discussed important psychological and spiritual problems, I told him how much I enjoyed playing patience—I mentioned the subject with some hesitation, for I thought he would consider it a pretty futile occupation! A few days later he wrote to me that he and his wife had started playing patience, and were finding it a very pleasant diversion.

We all have our fads and our failings. As the proverb says, no man is a hero to his valet. We all have our bees in our bonnets, our habits which we can no longer forsake, and that is not a little humiliating. Sometimes they are costly: how many husbands are there who are careful not to tell their wives how much they earn, in order to be able to hide from them (perhaps to hide from themselves) exactly what they spend on mediocre pleasures, while at the same time they exhort their wives to economize with the housekeeping money. And the wives often put down as 'groceries' the expensive beauty-products they are unable to resist the temptation to buy.

So we are all afraid of reality; we pretend to want to know ourselves, and we are afraid of knowing ourselves. Even when we consult them, we are always a little frightened of the graphologist, the psychotechnician or the psychiatrist. It is not only the picture that other people have of us that we are afraid of having to revise, but also the picture that we ourselves have of other people. For the young and adventurous frame of mind which is ready and eager to discover ourselves as well as others, we soon substitute the fatal pretension of knowing ourselves and knowing our neighbours. Many a husband imagines that he knows his wife, and as a result loses the loving curiosity he had while they were still only engaged to be married.

If we send the sick to hospital, the mentally sick to the mental hospital, the infirm to the Old People's Home, those with nervous complaints to the clinic, and difficult children to the reformatory, it is undoubtedly because they will be better cared for there. But it is also a little bit, whether or no we admit it, in order to remove from our sight these witnesses to human frailty. Civilized society does not like to see distress and poverty. Or rather, when they are revealed to it, there is a sudden and intense wave of sympathy (think of the success with which collections are made after a catastrophe), but the crowd soon turns its attention away from them; it does not care to meet them at every turn of everyday life.

The feeble, the infirm and the nervous are very acutely aware of this. They are capable of endless deception in order to hide their infirmity. Even a great grief, if it cannot help showing itself at first, is soon discreetly covered up, through a feeling that other, happier folk, ought not to be importuned by it. There is another deeper reason for this, which sets up a serious obstacle in the way of personal contact. Men are at bottom terribly conscious of their impotence when faced with great sorrows; and they do not like to be made to feel it.

A couple came to see us from a distant part of the country.

They had suffered the great sorrow of losing a child in tragic circumstances some weeks previously. Towards the end of the evening these friends began to tell us of their spiritual loneliness. Once the first few days had passed, in which they had received many tokens of sympathy, they had no longer been able thus to talk quite simply and openly of their grief. For great misfortunes raise many questions to which one does not know what answer to give.

The fear of not knowing what to say makes us talk of something else, divert the conversation on to subjects that are not so uncomfortable to discuss. I am sure that many doctors are often intuitively aware of the great life-problems which lie in the background of disease, but are careful not to touch them for fear of not knowing, were their patients to take them into their confidence, how to help them to solve well-nigh insoluble problems. And yet, in default of replies, our patients do at least need to be listened to.

Finally there is the fear of emotion. Many people avoid personal subjects through fear of the emotions they may arouse, for fear of weeping, of having their hearts touched and their sensitiveness revealed. They are afraid that such demonstrations might be taken for signs of weakness. A false feeling of shame about the emotions is very widespread. It is probable that the popularity of 'weepy' films is due to the need to give vent from time to time, in a place where it is not frowned upon, to the emotions which are kept in check in ordinary life.

At the bedside of a seriously ill person, whose days it seems are numbered, the doctor often (and even more often the family) goes out of his way to preserve in the patient the idea that he will get well. Of course that is because a cure is always possible, however improbable it may be, so long as life remains. And of course, too, it is to keep up the patient's morale. But sometimes the patient is not deceived, and his questions are hedged at, even when he possesses a spiritual maturity that renders him capable of consciously facing death. Is it not the supreme dialogue that those around him are thus avoiding? It is a dialogue which takes on a most moving solemnity in the perspective of the coming separation.

How many married couples no longer know how to tell each other quite simply that they love each other? Even joy is often smothered. Yesterday evening a mother announced to me the engagement of her daughter.

'You approve of the young man?' I asked.

'Oh, absolutely!'

'Then I hope you flung your arms round her neck and told her so.'

'No, I didn't dare to. I told her it was getting late, and she had better go to bed, and that we should talk about it some other time. . . .'

'You are implacable,' one of my patients said to me yesterday. 'But mind you', she added, 'that's why I come to see you.'

The reader will perhaps be thinking that I was pressing her with questions. Not at all: I was listening. I was listening with the intense attention that a struggling soul deserves. I sensed within her that inner struggle which I too know, the struggle to be really honest.

With all our hearts we aspire to become personal once more, to get rid of our personage, to find our person again and through it personal contact, fellowship. That aspiration comes up against a terrible obstacle within us. Her head bowed between her hands, my patient went on adding little by little, between long silences, some detail to her story. Without these details she knew well that there would be no liberation for her. It was then that she suddenly broke off to say:

'You are implacable . . . that's why I come to see you.'

There are no half-measures in this matter of honesty. One confidence leads to another, until even those which one finds most difficult to share come into one's mind. At that point one feels a sort of paralysis; one has a desperate longing to break off the dialogue. But how uneasy one feels about telling so much and yet not all. A life may be in the balance at that moment. What is required of us is that we should be implacable, but also that we should understand what is happening, that we should help that life lovingly to victory.

This may involve the calling back to mind of memories so painful that one has never been able to speak of them to anyone. For this reason they are doubly toxic: firstly on account of the ineffaceable wound they have caused; but also on account of their secrecy. There are secrets which can weigh on the heart to the point of crushing it. To tell them is to relive them, to experience all over again the intolerable emotion which has become attached to them, and which their secrecy is an attempt to hold at arm's length. A certain subject has become taboo; as soon as the conversation approaches it intense anguish is felt.

But on this road of honesty, towards the discovery of the person, there necessarily arises another type of memory—the memory of things for which one feels responsibility, which arouse a sense of guilt. 'Sin', writes Père Ducatillon, 'is eminently the act of the person.'[1] Here the obstacle is remorse, shame, the fear of being judged. The remedy is grace, which first helps us to overcome the obstacle and then effaces the sin.

I have often written about confession already, but misunderstandings still persist. The fear has been expressed by theologians that I am enlisting the doctor to take the place of the priest.[2] I have not done so, and never shall. That a Roman Catholic must seek sacramental absolution in the Confessional, that we must urge him to do so, and that he cannot excuse himself on the pretext that he has confessed to his doctor—all this is clear: one cannot make one's peace with God by cheating one's Church.

But the theologians must see things as they really are, and not as they would like them to be. There are all around us vast numbers of people who are sick for confession, even among Roman Catholics and Eastern Orthodox Christians, even among

[1] R. P. Ducatillon, O.P., 'Taille de l'homme pécheur', in *L'homme et le péché*, Plon, Paris, 1938.

[2] Abbé J.-P. Schaller, 'Les limites de la médecine et le docteur Paul Tournier', in *Bulletin de la Société médicale des hôpitaux*, Laval Médical, Quebec, April, 1954, p. 551.

those who go regularly and sincerely to confession and who may suddenly, in a personal conversation, realize that they are guilty of wrongs that are of much more decisive importance for their lives than any they have so far confessed.

Moreover there are those who have kept away from their Church precisely in order to escape confession, and who will be able to return to it as a result of the liberating hour spent with their doctor. And then there are the Protestants, among whom the practice of confession has fallen into grave disuse. Pastor Thurian has recently recalled[1] with what clear insistence the reformers enjoined the regular practice of confession. With great discernment he shows the importance of restoring it in the Protestant Churches. Like the Roman Catholics he accepts the religious validity of confession only when made to a minister of the Church, whereas the Orthodox Church recognizes confession made in the presence of a layman.

Lastly there are the unbelievers, the half-believers, the agnostics, and even those who are violently and aggressively anti-religious. They have as much need as believers of expressing their remorse. I do not suppose that any theologian expects me to break off the dialogue the moment it takes on the character of an exchange of profound confidences, for fear of usurping the place of the priest, especially since psychological factors may be intimately involved in genuine stirrings of conscience. In such a case—it is my duty to say this—the doctor has a part to play in which the priest cannot take his place.

I am not speaking here, then, of sacramental confession, which is the concern of the theologian. Dr Stocker has suggested[2] that in order to avoid all misunderstanding the term 'communication' should be used for confession in the doctor's consulting-room. I am therefore here speaking as a doctor and as a psychiatrist of this 'communication' as an event involving the soul, that event which is of all the most specifically personal. I am speaking in particular

[1] Max Thurian, *La confession*, Delachaux and Niestlé, Neuchâtel, 1953.

[2] A. Stocker, *Le traitement moral des nerveux*, Editions du Rhône, Geneva, 1945.

of the attitude of mind to which it bears witness. That attitude is quite simply that of complete honesty towards oneself and towards one's partner in the dialogue. Now it so happens that one is only completely honest with oneself if one is being so at the same time with God and with one's fellows. If I were a naturalist I might call it a 'law of the mind'. This, if I am not mistaken, is the same honesty which Dr Durand, at a conference of psychotherapists and theologians at the Ecumenical Institute, called 'psychological morality'.

It is its emphasis on responsibility which characterizes this confession, and which makes it an act of rebirth of the person. It is most striking, the way in which psychotherapists such as Dr Durand, and many others, who claim to be followers of Freud, that is to say of a quite mechanistic psychology which denies the concept of responsibility, are coming back, in spite of their theories, to stress the specific value of a sense of responsibility as a condition of the liberation of the person.

It is not necessary for me to insist on the medical value of confession. A bad conscience can, over a period of years, so strangle a person's life that his physical and psychical powers of resistance are thereby impaired. It can be the root cause of certain psychosomatic affections. It is like a stopper which can be pulled out by confession, so that life begins at once to flow again. That is why Dr Sonderegger called the doctor the 'natural confessor of humanity'; and why Michelet wrote that 'a complete confession is always necessary in medicine'. At the beginning of this century Dr Dubois, of Berne, who did not call himself a Christian, wrote: 'Confess your patient.'[1]

There you have the truly personal dialogue, which involves mutual commitment, in which inner freedom is to be found. This does not mean that we in our turn should make our patients our confessors. What is necessary is that we ourselves should take the road of confession, either sacramental or not, as our Church dictates, before we receive our patients—so that we can be free and able to speak simply, truly and personally, for without that

[1] *Op. cit.*

there can be no dialogue. Thus our ministry as confessors is intimately dependent upon our own experience of confession.

It is clear now why good will does not suffice to re-establish personal contact in the world of today. I often meet people who are as aware as I am of the extent to which our world has become depersonalized. They deplore the fact, but they do not see what religion has to do with it. Believing that a sufficient answer to the problem can be found in a humanistic philosophy, they do make sincere efforts to create a more personal spirit around themselves. I am glad of this, but I am persuaded that they are being utopian, and have not yet measured the enormity of the obstacle that has to be overcome.

The price that has to be paid for finding truly personal life is a very high one. It is a price in terms of the acceptance of responsibility. And the awareness of responsibility inevitably leads either to despair or to confession and grace. More is needed than the good intentions of the humanist. What is required is a new outlook, a personal revolution, a miracle.

The man who keeps secret his most painful memories, his bitterest remorse, and his most private convictions, must needs show also, in his whole demeanour and in all his relationships with other people, a certain reserve which they all intuitively feel. This reserve is contagious, and sets up an obstacle to the development of personal relationships. On the other hand, the liberation experienced by the man who has confessed his sins is also contagious, even if he says nothing about the burden that has been lifted from his shoulders. All who come into contact with him find themselves becoming more personal. In order to build a personal world we need persons, men reborn into a life of freedom and responsibility. This second birth is not the fruit of our own resolve, any more than our first birth was. It comes by grace, through the encounter with God, through dialogue with him.

9

THE LIVING GOD

L ET US SEE where we stand. We have seen that man runs
away from the dialogue for fear of discovering and revealing
his person as it really is. But we have also seen that he seeks
the dialogue, and awakens to personal life when he overcomes his
resistance and finds true contact with others. Then the person
emerges from the personage, not only in the dialogue of soul-
healing with a minister of religion, nor only in the psychotherapeutic dialogue with a doctor, but in ordinary life, in a
heart-to-heart talk with a friend, even in a fleeting exchange of
glances, if it has the note of authenticity.

This experience culminates, as we have just said, in confession,
when an individual surrenders his most intimate secrets, those
which are the most heavily charged with emotion or remorse.
Then it is that there takes place the great struggle against the
obstacle within. Let us examine what it is that is going on at this
point.

Whence does victory come? The atmosphere in which the
dialogue is taking place, the assurance of being loved and understood, is an important factor. But there is also an irresistible force
within, which compels us to be honest to the bitter end, to throw
off the mask of the personage and uncover the person.

When my patient is in the throes of this struggle, his almost
inaudible words broken by long silences, there is taking place
within him another, inner dialogue. This second dialogue is with
God, even if the man concerned is not a believer and thinks he is
wrestling only with himself. His whole being resists, as we all do;
if he speaks, it no longer comes from himself, but from a force
more powerful than he. It is God who is constraining him.
The woman I mentioned who said: 'You are implacable . . .',

was simply uttering aloud an answer from her inner dialogue.

There are then two parallel dialogues, two personal contacts—one with another person, the other with God. These two dialogues are closely interconnected, like the two great commandments, love towards God and love towards our neighbour, which Jesus declared to be alike (Matt. 22.37-40). So true is this that confession to God by oneself has no liberating quality, and that in prolonged isolation there is no dialogue with God. The very hermits need confessors. But, inversely, neither is there any real human dialogue unless it is, so to speak, doubled by an inner dialogue with God.

It is the latter which is important, which liberates, awakening and revealing the person. For the words which are exchanged between my patient and me have no significance apart from the inner movement of the soul which is taking place within us both and which is at this moment, for me as well as for him, personal contact with God. That is why at that moment silence can be even more valuable than words. We both find ourselves drawn into a relationship with God. There is between us the presence of God calling forth the person and establishing fellowship. At the end of such an interview the other day, in which neither of us had actually mentioned God, there came spontaneously to my lips the following remark: 'The whole of our conversation today was like a prayer, wasn't it?' That remains true even if my patient's beliefs differ from mine, and even if he is an unbeliever, or thinks he is. I am speaking here of the facts, not of their interpretation. There is a conflict between God's demands and man's resistance to them, a dialogue between the searching voice of God and the replies it demands.

Thus many people are in fact, even without being exactly aware of it, in dialogue with God; and that not only at the culminating point of confession, which we have chosen in order to see more clearly what is happening; but every time that their scale of values is called in question in the inner struggle, every time a man makes a reference to a standard of beauty, goodness and truth.

Man differs from the animals in that he asks himself questions. He asks them about the world and about himself, about the meaning of things, the meaning of disease and healing, life and death. He is conscious of his weakness, of his responsibility and of his short-comings, and he asks himself if there is any way out. I know that it is in fact God who puts these questions to him, that it is God who is speaking to him, even though he may not realize it. Faith consists only in recognizing who it is who speaks.

We shall find, therefore, that all we have said earlier about the human dialogue is true also of this dialogue with God which runs parallel to it and gives it its meaning and its value. This it is which gives to man his 'new dimension' which distinguishes him from the animals, and makes the dialogue a creative spiritual event—creative of the person. 'It is the spiritual', writes Dr Stocker,[1] 'which makes the person.' And Dr Maeder: 'Faith is essentially the affair of the person.' Dr Orelli's formula, 'The person—a dialogue,' takes on its full meaning: a dialogue with God, a personal encounter with the personal God, involving acceptance of responsibility for ourselves before him.

Like the human dialogue, this dialogue is seen to be intermittent. Even the greatest saints have their times of drought, when God seems to be afar off. But the important thing about these moments of communion with God is not that they happen but rarely, like flashes of lightning in the night, but that with all their solemn richness they do happen, and that they mean more for our whole life and person than years of automatic existence. These moments are decisive—in the full meaning of the term—in determining our future. They are the crossroads where we take a new direction. Our life thereafter will depend on them.

When we described the moments of contact with other people as decisive, that was because there was another dialogue underlying the human dialogue, coming into existence at the same time. In the other person who approaches us so closely that he becomes totally committed with regard to us, God himself is approaching us, and compelling us to commit ourselves also. I do not say that

[1] *Loc. cit.*

that other person actually speaks with the voice of God, but I do say that through this human contact God is showing us what it is that he has personally to say to us.

Further, these two dialogues may not always go strictly together. Like the two lanes of a dual carriageway, they may separate in order to rejoin later on. It does happen that we experience the encounter with God in solitude. But in that case it will have been prepared for by other human encounters, and it itself will be the preparation for still more encounters which will owe their depth to it.

Even when the Word of God strikes a man without warning, when there is a sudden conversion, an inner call, which changes all at once the direction of his life, he perceives that God has been speaking to him for a long time, that the dialogue was already going on in the darkness of the unconscious before it broke out into the full light of day. He realizes then that God is speaking to us all the time, through every thing and every person, that he speaks through the poets and musicians, through children and through the aged; through the example of the saints and through anyone he chooses, through the flowers and the beasts, in our dreams and in events.

He speaks to us doctors through the distress and suffering of our patients, through their confidences and confessions; he speaks in sickness and in healing, in joy and in sorrow. He speaks in parables, and when we understand this everything takes on new meaning, nature and history as well as every incident of our lives.

One of my patients tells me of an experience she has had this summer. Braving the displeasure of her mother, who wished to keep her beside her, and moved by a force she did not understand, she went off, deep into the heart of the country. There, as she lay in a meadow under the sun, she felt as never before a sense of communion with nature. She learned something of what the grace of God means. The reason why she is sitting in my consulting-room now is that that day changed the course of her life.

But it is above all through the Bible, the book of the Word revealed and incarnate, that God speaks, and personal contact with him is established. And when it is established, Bible-reading is no longer an irksome effort to solve an enigma as to absorb general precepts. It becomes a personal dialogue in which the least word touches us personally.

Why does the Bible so often speak of the 'living' God? Surely it is because the God it reveals to us is not the God of the philosophers, outside time and space, the origin of all things or the sublimest possible conception of the mind. He is a living person, a person whose voice breaks in upon us, who himself intervenes, who acts, who suffers, who enters into history in Jesus Christ, who enters into men by the Holy Spirit. We recognize in him the characteristics of life that we studied earlier—not so much motionless essence as movement, impulsion, guiding force.

At the same time the Bible reveals to us what the person is. Man is the being to whom God speaks, with whom he thus enters into a personal relationship. After having created the whole inorganic world, and all the plants and animals—a world blindly and impersonally subject to him—God created man in his image; that is to say, a personal being, a partner in dialogue, a being to whom he might speak and who could answer, to whom he gave liberty, and whose liberty, refusals and silences he respects, but whose replies he also awaits.

Pastor Bindschedler has devoted a recent study to the notion of the person in the light of the Bible.[1] The Bible always shows man as a unity, and always, in his totality, 'in his place before God'. The terms $\sigma\hat{\omega}\mu\alpha$ (body), $\sigma\acute{\alpha}\rho\xi$ (flesh), $\psi v\chi\acute{\eta}$ (soul or mind), $vo\hat{v}s$ (mind), do not in the Bible refer to distinct parts of man, attached together in some way, but 'always the whole person seen from a particular angle'. As for the $\pi v\breve{\epsilon}v\mu\alpha$ (the Spirit), neither is this used to designate a constituent part of man: 'By the $\pi v\breve{\epsilon}v\mu\alpha$ we understand the whole man as God speaks to him. . . . From that moment man becomes a Person, for it is a personal relationship into which he enters with God.'

[1] Jean-Daniel Bindschedler, *Le fondement théologique de la Médecine de la Personne*, Thesis, Faculty of Protestant Theology, University of Strasbourg, 1954.

So the Bible is the book of the men to whom God has spoken and who have listened to him. From end to end it is a dialogue, a succession of precise, concrete, living dialogues. The characteristics of the dialogue that we have already described are present here too: men seek it and flee from it, they both desire and fear it. Adam is afraid when God calls him in the Garden of Eden; Cain is afraid when God speaks to him; Moses is afraid before the burning bush; Isaiah is afraid in his vision; even the Virgin Mary is afraid when the angel Gabriel visits her; the Christmas shepherds are afraid.

For the dialogue with God is not a quiet recitative all the time: frequently it is violently dramatic. Look at the Book of Psalms: there is plenty of rebellion against God there. At a medical conference in Holland I remember Dr van Loon speaking of a fact that had struck him: when his patients attained that degree of honesty to which psychotherapy leads, many of them admitted that they were in revolt against God. That is my experience too; and with all my heart I rejoice when these rebellions are brought out into the light of day, out of the deceptive silence behind which they have been muttering in secret.

Do not let it be imagined that one must remain silent about one's feelings of rebellion in order to enter into dialogue with God. Quite the opposite is the truth: it is precisely when one expresses them that a dialogue of truth begins. I am reminded of the circumstances under which one of my closest friendships began. It was a man I scarcely knew. A little younger than I, he had just joined a students' society of which I was a member. We had both been appointed delegates of our branch to a conference of the Berne branch. We had arrived too soon, and were sitting for a while on the banks of the Aar. We were engaging in a trivial conversation, which he suddenly interrupted with a direct question to me: 'Now tell me what it is you have against me.'

Thus a personal relationship with God which is to lead to the closest intimacy may sometimes begin from a stormy explanation. A man who thought himself an unbeliever suddenly sees that he was holding aloof from God because his heart was full of complaints against him, holding him responsible for his misfortunes. By giving expression to his reproaches he becomes more sincere—and the dialogue can begin.

Sincerity is the *sine qua non* of the dialogue. Sincerity towards other people is difficult; it is difficult too towards God, but there at least the difficulty is only on our side. Here are a few lines from a letter I received recently:

'I often ponder over the nature of true human sincerity, true transparency. . . . It is a rare and difficult thing; and how much it depends on the person who is listening to us! There are those who pull down the barriers and make the way smooth; there are those who force the doors and enter our territory like invaders; there are those who barricade us in, shut us in upon ourselves, dig ditches and throw up walls around us; there are those who set us out of tune and listen only to our false notes; there are those for whom we always remain strangers, speaking an unknown tongue. And when it is our turn to listen, which of these are we for the other person's sincerity? That should make us think of God, who is not only One who says: "Listen to Me!" but also One who says: "I am listening to You." '

Telling God frankly what I have to say to him, and listening to what he has quite personally to say to me—this is the dialogue which makes me a person, a free and responsible being. It means being in fellowship with God, and that is faith. It is what the Bible calls 'knowing God', 'knowing his name'—that is to say his person, for the name is the symbol of the person. Even if it is only a fugitive moment, that moment is creative: the person awakes and emerges. It is as if the whole of the rest of the world becomes as nothing; this dialogue is all that matters. The personage I put on in ordinary life is no longer of any avail to me: God does not stop at the personage—he goes straight to the person.

People often say to me: 'I don't seem to be able to say my prayers; what ought I to do?' I reply: 'Talk to God as you are talking to me; even more simply, in fact.' St Paul writes that the truest prayer is sometimes a sigh. A sigh can say more than could be contained in many words. We must be careful therefore not to restrict the living and spontaneous reality of prayer within some rigid formula.

There are moments of silent adoration which constitute supreme fellowship with God, a dialogue, even though it may not be put into thoughts and sentences. There are sudden moments of joy that are more binding than promises. There are heart-rending cries that ring truer than praises learnt by rote. There are liturgical prayers, repeated since childhood, into which one so puts one's heart that they are more personal than extempore prayers that strain after originality. Our own personal experience can never be taken as the norm for other people. What matters is that our prayers should be living and sincere. Each of us has his own temperament; one is more intuitive, another more logical; one is more intellectual, another more emotional. The relationship of each with God will be marked with the stamp of his own particular temperament.

The reader will remember that in speaking of the human dialogue we distinguished two levels on which it takes place, one below the surface, the contact between persons, and the other on the surface, made up of our gestures and words, and bearing the stamp of our temperament. So with the dialogue with God: here too, profound personal contact is only experienced through the agency of the apparent dialogue which expresses it.

In the same way, what we call the voice of God, in the dialogue, is not an abstraction or an hallucination. I am often asked about this by people who are afraid of deceiving themselves, of mistaking the voice of their unconscious or of their own desires for that of God. Sometimes they do just the opposite, and impute to God the most provoking words possible, as if he took pleasure in antagonizing them. Of course one can be mistaken, and in this respect psychology can be a tremendous help. It explains, for example, how it is that a person who has always been thwarted by his father expects to be thwarted by God as well.

But the fear of deceiving ourselves can paralyse us, and it

is better to run the risk of making an occasional mistake than to break off the dialogue by means of which God may in time show us where we have gone wrong. We may hear the voice of God in a biblical passage which comes home to us personally, in the remembrance of a remark made by a friend, in a question which we put to ourselves, in a thought which comes to us when in his presence, sometimes when we least expect it.

I always remember one New Year's Eve. I had left my wife at home in order to spend the moment of midnight, in accordance with tradition, standing in the Cathedral square with the uncle who had brought me up. When I got back I found my wife overwhelmed and transformed.

'I have suddenly realized for the first time the greatness of God!' she told me.

As the bells rang out, telling of the inexorable and endless march of time, it had been borne in upon her that God was infinitely greater than she had ever imagined. The voice of God had spoken to her through the voice of the bells, and she had answered. Her answer could be read in her radiant face. It was a reply so clear and true that I in my turn was touched by it.

The greatest event in life had taken place: the personal encounter of Creator and creature, the dialogue between the voice of God, so great that it makes itself heard in every earthly sound, without any one of them ever sufficing completely to express it, and the voice of man, so weak that nothing he can say is adequate to the reply. It is an incredible dialogue, so disproportionate are the participants—and yet they are like, for God willed man to be 'in his image' (Gen. 1.27); they are both persons, capable of engaging together in dialogue.

We were very weary, my wife and I, at the time. For years I had devoted myself energetically to church work, where as everyone knows, one is always coming up against problems which seem trivial indeed compared with the task to be accomplished. And now, of a sudden, God was showing us his greatness, calling us out of the tangle of sterile arguments in which I had let myself be caught. During the year that followed he led us from experience to experience, to a renewing of our whole personal and professional life, calling us from ecclesiastical activity to a spiritual ministry.

We were both already Christians, but ours was not a very personal Christianity. We were so engrossed in his service that we had scarcely any time to listen to him. We have been taught to listen to him, at length, passionately and concretely. For us this dialogue has become interwoven with our dialogue together as man and wife, imparting to it its value and its richness. From reply to reply, in spite of all our misunderstanding, all our neglect, all our running away, all our stubborn silence, it has taken us further than we ever imagined possible.

There are many people like us, who speak to God in prayer, but hardly ever listen to him, or else listen to him only vaguely. Some people may find it a help to write down the thoughts that come to them during the times they set aside for prayer. It can help to make our prayers richer and more definite. Prayer grows like a living organism. It has all the characteristics of life, its directing force, its automatisms, its gropings, its fluctuations, its deviations, its regulating corrections, its growth in volume and strength. As Dr Maeder says, 'The practice of prayer gives us a sense of being engaged in a sort of dialogue with God.'[1]

I must point out here that prayer is quite different from the introspection of the private diary, just because it is a dialogue, because of the presence of that Other, God. This is the same difference as there is also between introspection and the psychotherapeutical cure, even when the psychotherapist remains silent. His presence changes everything. Many people mistakenly describe the psychoanalytical cure as introspection. Nothing is farther from the truth. In introspection we become buried in ourselves, in a solitude in which, as we have seen, the person vanishes. In dialogue, on the other hand, both that of psychotherapy and—even more—in the dialogue with God, the person is asserted and made more definite through the personal relationship that is established.

[1] *Vers la guérison de l'âme.*

It does sometimes happen that my prayers degenerate into introspection. I can soon sense the difference: I begin, in fact, to listen to myself more than to God, to concentrate on myself instead of on him. It is then that the human dialogue can help to revitalize the dialogue with God. Contact with other Christians, their witness, what they have to say about their own experience of the activity of the Holy Spirit, renews the quality of my own prayer.

So prayer is far from being the 'disorderly' monologue of introspection, of which Eugene d'Ors speaks, in which everything gets more and more muddled. On the contrary, apart from awakening and developing our love towards God, it is a sure road to the setting in order of our lives and the discovery of the person. For it is before God, who knows us and loves and forgives us, that we dare to see ourselves as we are. 'No one can look at himself', writes François Mauriac, 'except down on his knees, in the sight of God.'[1]

When we come, honestly and often, to keep this tryst with God, we discover the God of the Bible, the personal God who cares personally for us, who concerns himself with us in particular, who has numbered the very hairs of our head (Matt. 10.30). He does not only love all men in general, but each of us in particular. He concerns himself not only with our destiny as a whole, but with our every care. He speaks to all men, but has a word for each, calling us, as the prophet says, by our name (Isa. 45.4). That is what is meant by a personal relationship.

Dom Weisberger, who is a member of a religious order as well as a doctor of medicine, expresses it thus: 'To defend the person it is not enough to confine oneself to the specific nature of man as a composite mind-body, a reasoning animal. To defend the person is to defend man as being somebody, Jack Brown or Jill Smith, unique, incommunicable, irreplaceable, willed and loved by God, not as man in general, but as himself by name.'[2]

[1] François Mauriac, *Journal*, Grasset, Paris.
[2] Dom Weisberger, O.S.B., *La défense de la personne*, an address delivered to the Société de Saint-Luc de Belgique, Impr. Tancrède, Paris.

God speaks to us through the voice of the bells, and through the voice of his ministers. He speaks, as to Elijah, through the soft breath of the wind, and as to Job, through the clap of thunder. He speaks to us through our own thoughts when we submit them to Him, through our feelings and intuitions. We often ask him great questions to which he does not at once—or ever—reply. But he tells us day after day what we need to be told for the nurture and direction of our person. Grace is given drop by drop.

He does not speak in the same way to all. Nothing is more futile in this respect than to compare oneself with other people, to imagine that God is nearer to those whose notebooks are the first to be filled with beautiful thoughts. There again psychology can help us to get things clearer: those whose up-bringing has taught them to be always doubting themselves doubt also whether they are hearing God, and their doubt makes them deaf.

Nevertheless the Bible is realistic. It corresponds with our own experience: if it shows us how fruitful this dialogue is, it does not pretend that it is easy. The Bible might be called the story of the dialogue interrupted and the dialogue re-established. From its very first pages it shows us the tragedy of man. He has been created for this very dialogue, intimate and sustained, with God. He is homesick for it, but he only recovers it in snatches, always incomplete and imperfect. The Bible shows us that at the same time the human dialogue has also been disturbed. Man has entered into solitude.

All that we have seen, the impossibility of grasping the person in its full and naked reality, the impossibility of establishing complete contact of person with person, without the personage intervening like a shadow, now falls into place in the light of the biblical revelation. We live in a disordered world, and one of the aspects of this disturbance is that we are cut off from the current of life which ought to flow constantly and freely between God and us, and between us and our fellow-men, just as each cell of an organism is in constant humoral communication with the others.

Another aspect concerns the two characteristics of the person that we have noted, namely, choice and responsibility. The drama of human choice has been described by Sartre.[1] He shows us man forced to choose and at the same time incapable of choice. The philosopher sees in this the source of human anguish. On responsibility, Jacques Ellul, Professor in the Faculty of Law at Bordeaux, presented a penetrating study to the Third Protestant Medico-Social Congress of France.[2] To be responsible is to have to reply. This results from the fact that God speaks to man. Professor Ellul recalls the two great questions that God first put to men; when he said to Adam: 'Where art thou?' (Gen. 3.9), and to Cain: 'Where is Abel thy brother?' (Gen. 4.9). Man has no true answer to either of those questions.

If we translate them into the terms of this book, we see that they correspond with the two problems of the person and of personal relationship with others. 'Where art thou? Where is thy person?' As we saw in Chapter 4, the person eludes us; it remains always more or less hidden behind the personage. 'What hast thou done with thy brother, with the bond that united you?' As we saw in Chapter 8, contact is disturbed, it comes up against the greatest of obstacles.

In the light of the Bible, Professor Ellul goes on to show that Jesus Christ takes man's place and answers for him. He alone can reply. Jesus Christ takes human responsibility upon himself. This is one of the meanings of the Atonement, which Sartre misses. For God's questions, which leave us dumb, there are substituted the questions which Jesus puts to man: 'Lovest thou me?' (John 21.16). Here again we can put it in terms of this book: Jesus Christ alone is a person in the full meaning of the word: '*Ecce homo*' (John 19.5). He alone is a person without a personage, he alone fully takes up the dialogue with God and with men.

For Jesus Christ is the dialogue re-established. He is God

[1] *Existentialism and Humanism.*

[2] J. Ellul, 'Les fondements bibliques de notre responsabilité', in *Actes et Travaux du troisième Congrès médico-social protestant*, Bordeaux, Imprimerie Coneslant, Cahors, 1952.

coming to us because we cannot go to him. For the dialogue with God is substituted the more familiar and accessible dialogue with Christ, who is the daily food of the Christian. That is what Pascal meant when he wrote: 'Apart from Jesus Christ we know not what our life is, nor our death, nor God, nor ourselves. Thus, without the Scriptures, whose only object is Jesus Christ, we know nothing, and can see but obscurity and confusion in the nature of God, and in our own nature.'

The action of Jesus Christ in the re-establishment of the dialogue was described with great clarity by Henri Ochsenbein in his address to the Strasbourg Congress.[1] He illustrated man's situation by the analogy of a triangle. Placed at one of the angles, man finds himself in a double relationship: on the one hand with God, at the apex of the triangle, and on the other with his neighbour, at the opposite end of the base. 'But', he said, 'this relationship, for which we were created, has been broken.'

In the Bible the term $\sigma \acute{a} \rho \xi$ (flesh) denotes the fallen state of man. It is not, then, a matter of an 'inferior part' of man, opposed to a supposedly 'superior part', the $\pi \nu \tilde{\epsilon} \nu \mu a$ (Spirit). $\Sigma \acute{a} \rho \xi$ signifies 'the life of the whole man' without Christ, whereas $\pi \nu \tilde{\epsilon} \nu \mu a$ 'denotes the re-establishment in Jesus Christ of the unity created and willed by God, that is to say in which man ceases to exist in and by himself, and becomes the man of the re-established triangle, not an angelic being, but truly human, that is to say a person'.

Man has then passed from the $\psi \nu \chi \acute{\eta}$ or 'immanent, transitory life which can be destroyed', to the $\zeta \omega \acute{\eta}$ or 'life that is given, existing outside ourselves and eternal. This $\zeta \omega \acute{\eta}$ does not exist, for the Bible, outside Jesus Christ.'

Thus we see the whole of the New Testament to be the only answer to the problems we have studied in this book. In it we read the wonderful dialogues through which Jesus transforms the lives of those whom he meets, drawing out the person buried

[1] Henri Ochsenbein, 'Le problème de la santé et la vision biblique de l'homme', in *Santé et vie spirituelle, Actes du IVe congrès médico-social protestant français à Strasbourg*, Oberlin, Strasbourg, 1953.

beneath the personage, and revealing personal contact to them. We witness the growth of real community in the Early Church. Glossolalia, or speaking with tongues, which played such an important part then, and which is still found in some modern communities, appears to answer to the need of the Spirit to express the inexpressible, to carry the dialogue with God beyond the narrow limits of clearly intelligible language.

Christ is the re-establishment of contact. Through him to make contact again with God is to rediscover life, spontaneity, liberty and our fellow-men. Were we not saying just now that good intentions are not enough to heal our depersonalized world? We need redemption, the restoration through Christ of the dialogue. He is there, unseen but present, between my patient and me when we try to make contact, between God and me when I am seeking him. Christ is the personal God in very truth, the God who committed his person, even to the cross.

The other day I saw again an elderly maiden lady who has undergone, and is still enduring, very great suffering, but whose life is full of the radiant piety that comes from personal attachment to Jesus Christ. Each time she comes to see me I discover in her, in spite of the limitations that age and ill-health impose upon her, some new maturity, some new fruit of her life of prayer.

When quite young she lost her fiancé in tragic circumstances. At one blow all her joyous hopes of a home, husband and children crumbled away. Her faith upheld her, but the wound never healed. Now she tells me that through prayer she has come to see how in her trial she had shut up her heart against life; she had said 'No!' to the life which was denying her so much.

'Do you not think', she adds, 'that it is possible that that attitude compromised my health and my vitality?'

Do not misunderstand me: her life has been a fruitful one— fruitful in personal contacts and in spiritual children. And yet what she tells me now has an arresting ring of truth about it. In the intimate dialogue that she has with her Lord a new spring of life has welled up and overflowed the dam of her affliction.

She has been able to listen to the divine voice and reply to it. To say 'Yes' to God is also to say 'Yes' to life, even if it is a maimed and crippled life. It is to turn from the negative to the positive, for the call of God is positive.

Many people identify the voice of God with the voice of conscience. But it goes far beyond that, as I must now show. The voice of conscience is mainly remorse. It is true that the moral conscience, the psychology of which has been the subject of a penetrating study by Dr Baruk,[1] is a gift from God. And as such it is what confers upon man his humanity. But, if I may put it so, it is only the prologue to what God has to say to us, as our Lord's 'Repent ye', at the beginning of the Gospel, is only a prologue to all the rest of his teaching. 'The kingdom of heaven is at hand' (Matt. 3.2).

In the struggle I was describing at the beginning of this chapter, when a patient is painfully making his way towards a complete confession, absorbed in his inner dialogue, the voice of conscience says to him: 'You have sinned'; but the voice of God adds: 'Confess it.' One is negative, the other positive; one crushes, the other is a call to deliverance and to life.

I am over-simplifying. We have seen how the human person is not to be confined within the borders of any of the definitions we try to make of it. How much more does God refuse to be limited to a formula! Nevertheless I have felt it worth while to stress this contrast between the negative and positive voices, because far too many people stop at the first.

The voice of God is not heard only in reproof. And when he does reprove it is only in order to open the road that leads to liberation and action. He calls, he sends, he gives a purpose to life, he moves us, and thus awakens the person. As Professor Siebeck says: 'It is the calling that creates the person.'

God calls Amos (Amos 7.14-15), the insignificant herdman following his flock. He takes him out of his limited automatic life and makes him a prophet before the people and the king. Self-contemplation would never have led Amos to discover his

[1] *Op. cit.*

person. He reveals it as he answers God's call. Here once more we see the nature of life and of the person. They are not essences, but acts; not static, but dynamic.

Everywhere in the Bible we see men thus touched by the divine dialogue, so that they find their true dimension. Their stature increases, and bursts the seams of the cramped garment of the personage. We are here at the heart of the problem of the person. We can see why introspection failed. However carefully and candidly a man examines himself today, he will not find what God will awaken in him tomorrow. His person is not a fixed datum, but a potential, a development, a plan known to God, and he will lead him day by day towards its fulfilment.

Dr Aloys von Orelli speaks of this in his *Persönlichkeit, Selbst, Person*. He alludes to one of the notions of depth psychology, the 'id', which embraces the totality of human nature, and is therefore much more than the conscious 'ego'. He goes on to say that the notion of the person comprises, like the 'id', this totality, but adds to it the fact of a responsible relationship. 'This means', he writes, 'so to speak, a directed "id", which does not merely repose harmoniously in the universe, but which is in relationship with a second person, a "Thou" which confronts it and to which it is compelled to reply, towards which it is responsible.'[1] He adds further that the notion of the person is nowhere so clearly placed in the centre of the picture of man and the world as in the prologue of St John's Gospel: 'In the beginning was the Word.'

The Bible moves entirely in the perspective of a divine purpose and of a God who calls men to fulfil it, at the same time fulfilling their own personal destiny. Look at St Paul, the Pharisee, the doctor of the law, meticulously engaged in plumbing the Scriptures to find there the nature of God and of truth. Suddenly the dialogue breaks into being on the Damascus Road (Acts 9), and his life is transformed into an incredible adventure. He does not stop being a scholarly theologian, but he finds truth in action, fighting for Christ. In everything he writes we can hear the echo of the passionate dialogue in which he is daily engaged. He asks

[1] *Op. cit.*

for deliverance from an affliction, and God's answer is: 'My grace is sufficient for thee' (II Cor. 12.9). He desires to retrace his steps towards Asia, towards the familiar Churches, and God speaks to him in a vision; by the apparition of a Macedonian he calls him to go over into Europe (Acts 16.9).

Prayer constantly enlarges our horizon and our person. It draws us out of the narrow limits within which our habits, our past and our whole personage confine us. Sometimes we receive a clear command, whose implications we do not usually at first understand. It is only afterwards, as we look back over the road we have travelled, that we see that God had a purpose for us, and that he has compelled us to follow it in spite of ourselves.

The person is the divine plan of our life, the guiding force, itself directed by God, who leads us towards our vocation in spite of every deviation.

At some point on this journey we shall find that we have crossed a frontier: through personal fellowship with God we pass from the world of things to the world of persons.

PART FOUR

COMMITMENT

10

THE WORLD OF THINGS
AND THE WORLD OF PERSONS

I OWE THIS NOTION of the two worlds—the world of things and the world of persons—to Dr A. von Orelli, who developed it with telling effect at the Weissenstein medical conference. I shall not try to summarize his lecture here. To do so would demand of the reader a knowledge of the ideas and terms of depth psychology, or else it would require of me a skill in teaching them which I lack. But we can both readily understand the profound truth expressed in the idea of these two worlds.

There are two worlds, or ways of looking at the world, of entering into relationship with it, depending on the spirit in which we approach it. We may see in it nothing but things, mechanisms, from those of physics to those of biology and even of psychology. Art, philosophy, religion can also become things, collections of concepts, formulae, definitions. On the other hand, one can lay oneself open to the world of persons, awaken to the sense of the person. By becoming oneself a person one discovers other persons round about, and one seeks to establish a personal bond with them.

The person always eludes our grasp; it is never static. It refuses to be confined within concepts, formulae and definitions. It is not a thing to be encompassed, but a point of attraction, a guiding force, a direction, an attitude, which demands from us a corresponding attitude, which moves us to action and commits us. The world of things does not commit us. It is neutral, and leaves us neutral. We are cold, objective, impersonal observers, watching the operation of blind and inexorable mechanisms.

I am not claiming that we must shut our eyes to things, nor that we should cut ourselves off from intellectual objectivity, from the fascinating study of the ordinances and mechanisms of things. But I ask that we should not limit ourselves to the study of things, for they are only one half of the world, the static, impassible, unfeeling half. Even the heavenly bodies, moving with their unimaginable velocities, return in their orbits to the same position; this is the universal cycle of things, eternally starting again.

It is the person that has meaning, a birth and an end. The God of the philosophers is immutable; only the personal God has a purpose for history and for each being. To the scientist, man is but an episode in the universal dance of the atoms and the electrons. As the old French song says of the marionettes, 'Three little turns, and off they go!' Off they go to dance elsewhere in a purposeless round.

From infant school to university we are taught to know things, to isolate them, identify them, count them, measure them and classify them. There is no need for me to dwell on the enormous development that has taken place over the centuries in this field, so that now specialization within the narrowest limits is the order of the day. This has not been without its effect on our minds. They are becoming incapable of perceiving what is not objective.

In this depersonalized state of mind man himself becomes a thing. Anatomy and physiology study his body as a thing, and psychology his mind as a thing, a mechanism. Economics studies him as a thing, an instrument of production and consumption, while sociology studies him as an element of society. He is a pawn on the chess-board of politics, a cog in industry, a learning-machine, everywhere a fraction of the mass.

I have dealt with all this in Chapter 2, and need not go over it again. What I want to show now is how this unilateral view of the world and of man is completely upset by the awakening of the sense of the person. I mentioned a short time ago my own experience of this, when I turned from ecclesiastical activity to spiritual ministry, from technical to humane medicine. I was discovering the world of persons; I was discovering persons everywhere. Since that time, though I have not stopped being interested in things. I am much more passionately interested in persons.

I remember a visit paid to me by one of my former colleagues on the executive authority of the Church. I had fought him tooth and nail—that is to say, I had treated him as a thing, an adversary. The only thing about him that had mattered to me was his opinions, and the weight they might carry in the balance of our arguments. Ideas by themselves, detached from the person, are but things, abstractions, counters in the give and take of discussion.

And now here he was opening his heart to me. I too opened mine to him. He had come to talk to me about his personal life and his sufferings. I was making the discovery of his person, which I had never looked for before, I was so busy combating his ideas. I was discovering his person, his secrets, his solitude, his feelings. I even discovered that his ideas were not abstractions, but that they arose out of the sort of person he was, and protected his suffering like a shield. I talked with him about my own personal experiences, and realized that this former adversary had the same needs and the same difficulties as I, the same longing to find life and fellowship again.

With my patients I had one surprise after another. My knowledge of the mechanisms of their diseases remained unaltered. But I began to see that these diseases had a meaning in their lives, that they were not mere impersonal accidents, unwanted garments, but that they had something to do with their persons, that they were an expression of them.

A man may spend years in an office, seeing in his employees only their work, their good qualities and their failings, and then, when personal contact is established, suddenly discover what lies behind the façade: the secret sufferings, the sequels of unhappy childhood, disappointed hopes, struggles to remain faithful to ideals. Then too he may understand the profound significance of the qualities and failings he has seen, and the meaning that work can have when it is no longer a thing but the activity of a community of persons.

It is as if a light had shone on life and shown it up in new colours. 'We live', wrote Saint-Exupéry, 'not on things, but on the meaning of things.' The meaning of things is of the order of the person. When our eyes are opened to the world of persons, things themselves become personal. It is just the reverse of the transformation of men into things of which we were speaking just now. Beasts, plants and inanimate things take on the quality of persons.

All we possess, all we love, all we meet is incorporated into our person, shares in our person and takes on meaning through this personal sharing. One of my patients is a man who, in the most tragic circumstances during the war, experienced a sudden re-orientation of his spiritual life. He describes to me in striking terms what he felt at that moment. It seemed to him that everyone he met was a part of his own destiny. I sense, as he speaks, that he still bears the decisive imprint of that revelation. Love, he tells me, is something quite different from what is usually supposed. What people commonly call love is a mere function of sense, an emotional attraction. But since the change in his own life of which he is telling me he has seen it as a personal sharing in the destiny of another person.

When we have discovered this incorporation of people and things into our own person, we see it also in others. Things then are no longer things—they become transparent: no longer screens which hide persons, but living signposts which point us to them. The world comes alive; it speaks, and we enter into dialogue with it.

I remember that when we were discussing this at Weissenstein one of my colleagues recalled the great figure of St Francis of Assisi, and how he conversed with the beasts, with the wolf and the birds, and with Brother Sun. St Francis had himself become so fully a person, found such personal fellowship with God, that in every thing he saw a person, a reflection of the person of God.

Here is what Chesterton wrote of him:

'St Francis deliberately did not see the wood for the trees. It is even more true that he deliberately did not see the mob for the men. . . . He only saw the image of God multiplied but never monotonous. To him a man was always a man and did not disappear in a dense crowd any more than in a desert. He honoured all men; that is, he not only loved but respected them all . . . there was never a man who looked into those brown burning eyes without being certain that Francis Bernardone was really interested in him; in his own inner individual life from the cradle to the grave; that he himself was being valued and taken seriously. . . .'[1]

I am reminded also of Brother Lawrence, so keenly sensitive to the presence of God in all things.[2] There proceeds from such men an infinite poetry which touches us personally. For poetry depends on personal relationship with things, on an engagement of the self towards things. The whole of art—and of religion too— is of this quality. This is so at least with true art and true religion, as it is with true love. Do we not speak of the object of art, of God as the object of religion, of the sex partner as the object of instinct? Object comes from objective, and signifies thing. Thus everything with which we come in contact takes on the tone-quality of thing or of person, according as to whether we are ourselves a thing or a person in respect to it.

To become a person, to discover the world of persons, to acquire the sense of the person, to be more interested in people as persons than in their ideas, their party labels, their personage, means a complete revolution, changing the climate of our lives. Once adopted, it is an attitude which rapidly impregnates the whole of our lives. While at the Weissenstein conference I had occasion to congratulate one of my colleagues who had made an extremely good job of interpreting a talk I had given earlier in the day. 'And do you know why?' he asked me. 'It had been

---

[1] G. K. Chesterton, *St Francis of Assisi*, Hodder and Stoughton, London, p. 110.

[2] Brother Lawrence, *The Practice of the Presence of God*, S.C.M. Press, London, 1956.

mentioned to me that one of our Scandinavian friends was finding it very troublesome following the speeches in foreign languages. So I interpreted for *him*; I never took my eyes off him, watching his face all the time to see if he had understood. And I found that through giving more attention to his person than to the ideas I was translating, I actually found it easier to express the ideas.'

He had become an interpreter of the person, just as one can be a doctor of the person, or a teacher of the person, when one does not teach that impersonal thing, the class, but the persons of the pupils. In the same way, at a conference, one speaks quite differently if the audience is no longer an anonymous mass, if one seeks in it a few faces and exchanges glances with individuals, so that one's speech takes on the quality of a dialogue.

In the world of persons all one's professional relationships take on a new character. They become shot through with a joy that was absent when they were merely the fulfilling of a function. Everything becomes an occasion for personal contact, a chance to understand others and the personal factors which underlie their behaviour, their reactions and opinions. It is much more interesting, as well as important, to understand why someone has a certain failing, than to be irritated by it; to understand why he maintains a certain point of view than to combat it; to listen to confidences than to judge by appearances.

The atmosphere of office, workshop or laboratory is rapidly transformed when personal fellowship is established between those who previously criticized or ignored each other. In a recent lecture Professor F. Gonseth,[1] professor of philosophy at the Zürich Polytechnic, the pioneer of the review *Dialectia*, spoke of the 'law of dialogue' which he believes must govern the university of the future. By this phrase he means personal contact between teacher and student, so that the person is committed in the intellectual dialectic. The condition of this contact and

[1] F. Gonseth, a lecture delivered in Geneva, 27th November 1950, reported in *La Suisse*, 28th November 1950.

commitment is that the teacher should not be so absorbed in his subject that he forgets all about the persons to whom he wishes to transmit it.

I do not think that in order to initiate medical students into the medicine of the person we must necessarily make it the object of special courses of tuition. It is not taught, but caught. It requires personal contact between teachers and students, the teachers being men who are sensitive to the world of persons. Happily there are still some of these left in all our medical schools, and among them are some of the foremost men in the profession. The influence of such men affects our whole career.

Large numbers of doctors are concerned about the way modern medicine is evolving. While rejoicing unreservedly to see its prodigious scientific and technical progress, they seek to guard against the accompanying dangers, such as over-specialization, the gradual disappearance of the family doctor, and a certain standardization and mechanization of medicine attendant upon the rise of systems of social security, all of which increase the risk that medicine will lose its humane and personal character. It may well be that the extraordinary increase at the present time in the numbers of unqualified practitioners of all kinds is due in part to the growing impersonality of official medicine. It is estimated that in France, alongside the 38,000 registered doctors, there are 41,000 quacks and other unqualified practitioners.

Many doctors today are seeking means of correcting this disequilibrium. They know that good medical practice does not depend only on the technical competence of the doctor, but also on his personal influence. Medicine is still, as Georges Duhamel put it, a 'singular colloquy'. So we are beginning to hear everywhere of attempts to define and propagate the medicine of the person. Professors of medicine allude to it in their inaugural lectures, whether they occupy chairs of surgery like Dr Verdan,[1]

[1] Claude Verdan, 'De l'indication à l'acte opératoire', in *Revue médicale de la Suisse romande*, Lausanne, 25th March 1952.

of psychiatry like Dr Delay,[1] or of hospital practice like Dr Mach.[2] Such unanimity is symptomatic of the great need that is felt for synthesis in medicine. It is not of course entirely new. Dr Neubauer points out[3] that it was Socrates who said: 'The reason for the frequent failure of Greek doctors is their inadequate knowledge of the whole, the health of which is a necessary condition of that of the part.'

Now, the medicine of the person can be conceived as a grandiose science integrating, if not in a single super-expert, at least in a college of experts, all the knowledge acquired in every branch of medicine. This is the idea put forward by Dr Carrel at the end of his book *Man, the Unknown*.[4] One can easily imagine the tremendous advantages and interest of such an effort. But one can imagine the difficulties, too. Specialization creates in each branch a technical jargon which other doctors, because of their own specialization, find it difficult to follow.

We see it happening already in our international conferences on the medicine of the person. Often, for instance, surgeons and psychiatrists have expressed to me their appreciation of these meetings, in which they can talk to each other about their own experiences, whereas in the usual type of scientific meeting they find themselves only with specialists in the same branch as themselves. But a surgeon will also confess how difficult he finds it to follow a lecture by a specialist in depth psychology, while the latter will similarly admit that he finds it hard to grasp the point of view of a surgeon.

Consider then the situation if to these various kinds of doctor we were to add educationists, sociologists, philosophers, historians and theologians, who have all a contribution of their own to make to our knowledge of the human person, but who all have

[1] Jean Delay, 'Inaugural Lecture', in *La Semaine des hôpitaux*, 14th October 1947.

[2] René-S. Mach, 'Inaugural Lecture', in *Praxis*, Berne, No. 1, 1954.

[3] Vinzenz Neubauer, *Der Weg zur Persönlichkeit*, Tyrolia Verlag, Innsbruck-Vienna, 1947.

[4] Alexis Carrel, *Man, the Unknown*, Penguin Books, Harmondsworth, 1948.

their own specialized language. Moreover, many divergences exist even among leaders in the same field of specialization. Take for example the bitter antagonism that exists between the various schools of analytical psychology. Each has made important discoveries and furnished us with valuable concepts; but the conceptions of the human person which each deduces from them are utterly different.

It is easy, therefore, to gather together a vast amount of knowledge about man, but singularly difficult to arrive at a synthesis of it. Such a medicine of the person would be inaccessible to the ordinary practitioner, who nevertheless needs practical help in the task of making medicine more humane. Moreover, all that we have seen in the course of this book makes us doubt whether this is really the way to an understanding of the person. Even if I could arrive at a knowledge of all the physical, chemical and biological phenomena of the body, all the psychical phenomena of the mind, and all the spiritual, social, historical and philosophical factors at work in man, would it make me into a doctor of the person? Would it result in personal contact with my patient?

In the end of the day I should still be in the world of things. Knowledge of things, even of an infinity of things, does not bring us to knowledge of the person. Do not misunderstand me: I am not denying the usefulness or the interest of the effort to synthesize our scientific knowledge of man. But however successful, it will reveal only one side of man's nature, that of his mechanisms. It will still be necessary to complete it with a personal knowledge, which is of a different order, the order of the person, not that of things. This knowledge is within the reach of every doctor, be he an ordinary general practitioner or a learned specialist.

The prime necessity, then, for the medicine of the person, is that we should open our hearts to the world of persons, learning to see our patients not only as the scene of this or that phenomenon, but as persons. And that depends not so much on the knowledge we have accumulated as on our own evolution as persons. As one theologian has said: 'It is by becoming persons ourselves that we discover the persons of our fellow-men.'[1] That is what Dr Paul Plattner means when he writes: 'The medicine of the person invites every doctor to an inner renewal.'[2]

For me as a doctor to become a person, to attain completeness as a human being, the road is the same as for my patients, and I must commit myself to it before I can hope to lead them along it. It is the road of personal dialogue with God and with my fellows. There is a decisive turning I must take, that leads me out into the world of persons, at one of those decisive moments of which we have spoken. But there is also a daily becoming, a constant casting aside of my personage, a constant renewal of personal contact with God and with my neighbour.

It is this aptitude for personal contact, which is created and nourished by being sincerely sought after, which is proper to the medicine of the person. Through it I become myself a person, and at the same time help my patient to become one. Our relationship changes from that of doctor and client to become that of partners in a dialogue. There comes into being a 'reciprocity of consciousness', to use M. Nédoncelle's admirable expression.[3] I allow my person to be discovered and known, and at the same time discover and know the person of my patient. It is in this that the medicine of the person demands a personal commitment which is not called for by technical medicine.

It is a new attitude, which depends on me as much as on my patient. Let me illustrate this from what happened with one of my patients. She had lived in extreme spiritual isolation, and was so afflicted by timidity that our first few conversations were very laborious indeed. She was burning to unburden herself to me, but could not bring herself to do so. She answered my questions in monosyllables. Suddenly, one day, all that was

[1] Charles Hauter, 'Les deux natures en Christ', in *Revue d'histoire et de philosophie religieuses*, 1952, No. 3, p. 201, Presses universitaires de France, Paris.
[2] Paul Plattner, *Médecine de la personne*, Artsenblad, Amsterdam, April, 1950.
[3] Maurice Nédoncelle, *La réciprocité des consciences*, Aubier, Paris, 1942.

changed. She did not notice it herself, for she seemed taken aback when, at the end of the interview, I remarked to her:

'Well, the miracle happened today, didn't it?'

After a moment's thought she replied:

'It's quite true, I was able to speak freely.'

Personal contact was established.

But from then on, contact depended as much on me as on her. It could be lost again. And that is just what happened. The other day our conversation became heavy again. After she had gone I was saying my prayers, and God showed me that it was I who was responsible: I had allowed myself to be hurt by a reproach she had made to me. Of course I had not let her see it—I had not even been aware of it myself, preoccupied as I was with justifying myself by means of grand theories. In short, the personage had reappeared in me to hide the wound caused in the person. It needed the dialogue with God for me to be shown what had happened, and for personal contact to be re-established by means of a sincere letter. The more a person opens his heart to me, the more important is it that he should find in me a man in close contact with God.

Many writers have stressed the vital importance of the person of the doctor, of the quality of his personal life, of his honesty with himself, with God, and with his patient. Dr Armand Vincent of Paris,[1] Dr Alphonse Maeder of Zurich (in numerous publications),[2] Professor Ramón Rey Ardid of Saragossa,[3] and many others besides, have all come to this same conclusion, that what characterizes the medicine of the person is the person to person contact between doctor and patient.

At the Weissenstein conference, Professor R. Siebeck of Heidelberg examined the question of how a personal medicine could be practised in the impersonal atmosphere of the hospital.

---

[1] Armand Vincent, *Le jardinier des hommes*, Editions du Seuil, Paris, 1945.

[2] See in particular *La personne du médecin, un agent psychothérapeutique*.

[3] Ramón Rey Ardid, *El sentido religioso de la medicina de la persona*, Octavio y Félez, Saragossa, 1953.

There the patient is in much greater danger than in the consulting-room of being allowed to feel that he is a mere thing, a case, a number. There are many measures that can be adopted, which I have no space to enumerate here. But he stressed that the most important thing is the person of the medical superintendent himself, the spirit which animates him in his relationships, not only with the inmates, but with his fellow-workers, the doctors, assistants, matron and nurses.

Professor Siebeck spoke of a certain nurse whose mere presence sufficed to create, everywhere she went, a personal atmosphere. I have often heard of similar examples. There are people—person-ages—who create an impersonal atmosphere around themselves; but if someone is truly personal, those who are near him feel themselves to be persons.

A doctor who has no personal contact with his wife will seek in vain such contact with his patients. Our life is subject to an inexorable law of unity. Either we move in the world of things, phenomena, personages, and God himself is just an abstract idea; or else we enter the world of persons; God becomes personal; we meet persons everywhere, in the intimacy of the home as well as in those great impersonal machines we call hospitals.

I was with some friends one day, and they were advising me to give more lectures and write less books, for, they said, in my writings they missed the personal accent of the spoken word. As you see, I am not following their advice. However precious one's friends are, one must not become their slave. Being a person means acting according to one's personal convictions, due regard of course being given to those of others. And my friends' observation is true. The living word remains the chief instrument of personal dialogue.

This is clearly seen in the case of those patients who send me beforehand—in writing—a long account of their lives. This is useful as information. But the point is that the purpose of a life-history is not so much to furnish information as to lead towards personal contact. Given by word of mouth it may be less intelligible, less systematic, but it is a method which calls for a much deeper commitment of the person.

I have my patients who write me letters after each consultation. They put in them the things they have not dared to say to my face. This has its value; it is for them a commitment, a way of forcing themselves to become more personal at the next consultation. But it is also a means of sparing themselves the intense emotion of a verbal explanation. It attenuates the dialogue, making it less direct because it uses a thing—paper—as an intermediary.

But even the spoken word itself can become a thing if it adopts the neutral and objective tone of information or discussion. Paradoxical though it may seem, the true dialogue is by no means a discussion. This is my answer to those of my colleagues who are perhaps afraid of not knowing what to reply to a patient who puts to them some moral problem that is on his conscience. It is important here to make a distinction between intellectual argument and personal encounter. Answer ideas with ideas, but answer the person with the person. Then often the heart's true response is silence.

Engaging in the dialogue, in the sense in which we understand it here, does not mean plunging into religious or philosophical theories about life, man, or God. The people who have helped me most are not those who have answered my confessions with advice, exhortation or doctrine, but rather those who have listened to me in silence, and then told me of their own personal life, their own difficulties and experiences. It is this give and take that makes the dialogue.

If we answer with advice, exhortation or theories, we are putting ourselves in a position of superiority, not equality. We are concerning ourselves with ideas, and not with the person, confining ourselves to the objective world of things, instead of entering the subjective world of persons. When someone lays bare to me the burning reality of his life, I am well aware that most of my replies could easily be only those of my personage. This is especially the case when a man expresses feelings of rebellion against the circumstances of his life, or his religious doubts. To give way to the urge to refute what he says would be to set up the personage of a so-called believer against that of a so-called unbeliever. It would be a denial of Christ's teaching that in the Kingdom of God the 'first shall be last' (Mark 10.31).

The moment the personage reappears, with its systems of thought and its claim to possess and express truth, our sincerest efforts to help others will finish by crushing and repressing them instead of liberating them. The dialogue between persons is replaced by a moralizing or proselytizing discussion. 'Those who impose upon us their ready-made solutions', writes one of my patients, 'those who impose upon us their science or their theology, are incapable of healing us.'

You will see now how wide of the mark are those who describe the medicine of the person as 'religious psychotherapy', in the belief that it consists in the indoctrination of the patient, denunciation of his failings, in moral uplift, or in exhorting him to accept his lot, and forcing him into confession and prayer. That indeed would be acting as a personage and not as a person. Then we should really be in danger of usurping the place of the minister of religion, and attempting to perform a function which is not proper to us.

It may well be the mission of the priest to warn, to correct, and to teach doctrine. It is not that of the doctor. Consider the case of a woman patient who, being a Protestant, is attracted by Roman Catholicism. But she is not clear in her own mind; in spite of all her admiration for the Roman Church she has been unable to come to a decision definitely to go over to it. The conflict tears her mind in two; it plays a clearly pathogenic role in her. It is constantly aggravated by her visits to pastors and priests, each of whom attempts to persuade her of the truth of his own doctrines while criticizing those of the other side.

What good should I do if I in my turn joined in this theological debate? Would I help her by imposing my Protestant beliefs on her while some Roman Catholic colleague did the same with his

Catholic ones? As a matter of fact she has also consulted a friend of mine, a Roman Catholic psychotherapist, and he did not urge her to go over to Rome any more than I press her to remain a Protestant. What she needs is to be able to talk to him, as to me, without being dragged into controversial discussion, so that she can lay before us her inner conflict as it appears to her.

Indeed, in the psychologist's eyes it is not so much a matter of a hesitation between Protestantism and Catholicism as between the pictures she has in her own mind of each. Underlying her hesitation are factors of her personal life and associations of ideas which it is necessary to understand and to help her to understand. In this way she may be led towards a really personal conviction, and meanwhile be enabled to bear the pain of doubt and hesitation with less injury to her person.

For one individual who is conscious to the point of obsession of his hesitations, how many more are there who are divided, not only between Protestantism and Catholicism, but between Christianity and other religions, or between faith and doubt, without being able to admit it clearly to themselves? It is by taking an interest in them as persons, in that growth of the person which takes place in the personal dialogue, that one can help them towards self-knowledge and sincerity in their religious life. How many are there for whom their religion is no more than a collection of spiritual automatisms resulting from upbringing or habit? We become persons only by making a personal decision.

The medicine of the person demands unconditional respect for the person of others. That does not mean putting one's own flag in one's pocket, but rather that we must state our convictions in a way that is truly personal, not theoretical, having at the same time a sincere regard for the convictions of others. In this way dialogue becomes possible where previously it has been shipwrecked on the rocks of religious, philosophical, political or social prejudice.

This, in my view, is not only a matter of tolerance, in the sense in which that word is usually understood, implying a certain claim to possession of the truth while condescending to live with those who are in error without persecuting them. It is a much more profound conception, arising from what we have said about the dialogue with God. That dialogue is essentially personal —and that implies that we seek in it guidance for ourselves, and not for others.

Obviously I am not referring here to dogma or to the God-given duty of the Church to preach his Word to men; nor yet to the authority over men's souls entrusted to the Church's ministers. I am speaking of the practical duty of seeking daily after God's will, to which all are called who have been enlightened by the Word of God, through the Church's teaching and the Holy Spirit. Thus it behoves me, and not others on my behalf, to listen to what God says to me personally, and so to forge for myself, as sincerely as I can, my own personal convictions. Conversely, it is no part of my duty to pass on to my fellows guidance supposedly received from God by me on their behalf.

I received recently from a friend abroad a questionnaire on various problems of the relations between medicine and faith, for a medical study-group. One of the questions was whether the doctor ought to tell his patient what he believes to be the spiritual significance of his illness. I answered in the negative. The spiritual meaning of events is in my view an essentially subjective notion. My business is the meaning of my own illnesses, not those of my patients. If I claimed to judge what is the meaning of other people's illnesses, I should in reality be setting myself up as a judge of the sick people themselves.

In any case I do not think that for the doctor to take such a course would be very fruitful. A spiritual experience like the discovery of the meaning of things, of what God is saying to the patient through his illness, must spring from within, from his inner dialogue with him. On the other hand, when he has had this experience he must be able to talk about it to his doctor and to find in him a whole-hearted respect for the convictions that have been born within him. This then is the personal dialogue, in which each expresses his own convictions rather than discussing those of other people.

Dialogue is my job. I happened one day to be at a meeting of psychotherapists and theologians. Each of my colleagues was defining himself as belonging to this or that school of thought. Having no label of that sort I conceived the idea of declaring that I belonged to the Socratic school. What I meant by this was that I adopted that method of frank dialogue which Socrates practised. Socrates, so far from imposing his own ideas on others, sought to help all who came into contact with him to see themselves more clearly and to acquire personal convictions.

This is something that goes far beyond 'psychotherapy', which term ought to be reserved for the specialist technical treatment of neurosis. Of course I do occasionally use such treatment, and the dialogue may well form part of it. But it is much more that that. It is an aid to life which every doctor can use without being a psychotherapist, with those who suffer from tuberculosis or heart-disease, and also with those who are well. They all need to be helped to live, to become persons, men in the full sense of the word. Such a transformation contributes in all of them to the safeguarding or the restoration of health.

Dr Gerrit van Balen of Bois-le-Duc once wrote to me that in his opinion the term 'neurosis' was being misused. It should, he said, be reserved for the true neuroses, obsessional neuroses, anxiety neuroses, abandonment neuroses, for all of which specialist treatment is required. But it is important that the label 'neurotic' should not be applied indiscriminately to any individual suffering from serious conflicts which make it necessary for him to ask a doctor for this aid to life. In such cases it is not the psychotherapist in us that they are looking for, but the man, a partner in real human dialogue.

Of course the mechanisms studied and described by psychologists are at work in such people, as they are in us all. To enlighten them on this point is as useful to them as to us. But they are no more sick than we are, or perhaps it is we who are as sick as they. And they are legion; they make up at least half of the clientele of every doctor, these people whose troubles both physical and psychical are but the expression of a conflict of life that has become too acute. Put us in the same circumstances, and we should be as 'ill' as they are.

It often hurts them to find themselves too readily labelled 'neurotics', or even when we approach them in our capacity as psychologists rather than as human beings, looking upon them rather as the seat of psychological mechanisms than as persons. Thus our psychological training, our science, the professional habits they form in us, our way of looking at man, can become obstacles to personal contact. We have acquired all this equipment in order to be better able to help people, and yet it can become a cloak under which our person disappears, and we become in-human professional personages.

Even in the treatment of a neurosis a moment comes when it behoves us to throw off this technical mentality in order to become a person again. I was vividly reminded of this one day by a remark made by one of my patients. Before her case was entrusted to me she had undergone a course of psychoanalysis from which she had derived great benefit. Excellent personal contact had been established with the doctor concerned. But she always felt that the moment she let slip any spontaneous remark in his presence, she knew the psychological label he was about to attach to it; according to her, her doctor analysed her every reaction, seeing each as an infantile regression, a mechanism of projection, of concealment, or of affective transfer.

So, although psychology is capable of removing the moral labels which cause so much suffering, it can itself seem to be passing judgment. For the man who has always been written off as lazy, to realize that his so-called laziness is but the expression of a repressed revolt against his parents, is a tremendous relief. He is delivered from a moral condemnation which he has always intuitively felt to be unjust. But now, if he can no longer lounge about without feeling that people are looking upon it as a psycho-pathological symptom, he experiences a sense of judgment.

Psychology is to the doctor a wonderful school for human understanding, a road towards contact, because it sweeps away prejudices. But if the personage of the psychologist in us takes precedence over the person, psychology can become a distorting mirror. If we are too ready to distinguish in people's behaviour the psychological mechanisms that are at work, we no longer see persons, but marionettes. We need to recover a certain naïvety in our approach.

The dialogue, personal contact—do they not belong in some measure to the Kingdom of God, of which Christ said that only those who become as little children shall enter therein? (Matt. 18.3).

11

TO LIVE IS TO CHOOSE

A YOUNG WOMAN comes into my study. She explains to me that she is suffering from stomach trouble, and that she has consulted a dozen doctors, from her village G. P. to specialists in the city and the hospital, being sent from one to the other.

'They tried to reassure me', she said, 'they told me it wasn't serious, that it was just nerves. But that didn't make me better.'

'Just nerves.' There indeed is the easy, misapplied label we were speaking of just now. It misleadingly suggests that this woman must attend to her nerves, whereas she is certainly in the throes of some inner conflict. It is this conflict that must be unravelled. But what is the conflict? Perhaps she herself does not know. Doubtless it will be a long and difficult task to uncover it, and even more so to resolve it, and I have but little time to spare. All this is going through my mind as she is speaking to me.

'How old are you?' I ask her.

'Thirty-six.'

'But you look at least ten years younger!'

'Yes, everyone says that I look very young.'

'I wonder why that is? There must be some reason.'

That is how the sense of the person awakens in us a new curiosity, a desire to understand not only the mechanisms of the details, on the scale of each separate organ, but the meaning of the whole, on the scale of the person. For the body is an expression of the person. If it seems younger than its age, that is because the person has not developed freely.

But my patient has not understood my question properly. I must try to make myself clearer:

'Do you think that some person or thing has prevented you from growing up?'

There is a long silence, while the woman sits lost in thought. At last she says to me:

'Do you mean my mother? She always treats me as if I were still a little girl.'

Mothers who prevent their children from growing up are not necessarily bad mothers, careless of their maternal duties, self-centred or authoritarian. They are often excellent mothers, keenly desirious of bringing up their children well and saving them from the errors and disappointments of life, sheltering them from its risks; mothers who give their children so much good advice that they become timid and unable to make up their own minds. They dare not make the responsible choice which, as we have seen, is one of the characteristics of personal life. So the flow of life is arrested.

The door is open for confidences: my patient tells me that she has already twice been engaged to be married, but that each time, as the date fixed for the wedding approached, her mother fell ill, and she put it off.

'It's my duty to look after my mother, isn't it? I could hardly leave her just when she needed me most.'

Each time, the man concerned had grown weary of waiting, and had broken off the engagement. Now—as I guessed—she is engaged for the third time; the date of the wedding is approaching, and her mother is getting less and less well.

The biblical precept is well known: 'Therefore shall a man leave his father and his mother, and shall cleave unto his wife' (Gen. 2.24). I explained this to my patient. Marriage, like every other vital act, demands a radical choice. She must choose between her mother and her fiancé. I summoned the latter to my consulting-room, and begged him to insist, come what might, that the wedding should not be postponed. I wrote a long letter to the mother, which she took very well. The young woman came to see me a few months after her marriage; the stomach trouble had gone, and her mother was in good health.

The doctor's first task is to heal. In some cases measures of a technical nature only are needed. But with many patients the doctor's task can only be fulfilled by his accepting a wider mission, an educative one. He is called upon to help people to develop, to re-enter the main stream of life by conforming to the laws of life, to grow up harmoniously, to become adult. This is in any case the true aim of technical medicine also: the removal of every physical and psychical obstacle to the growth and development of the person, so that its purpose in life may be accomplished. The gates of a level crossing are opened not because the man in the signal box likes opening them, but so that the cars can pass through. So the use to which health is put when it is regained is of even more importance than the health itself.

This is what we have termed an aid to life. It demands only a knowledge of the laws of life, the first of which is the need to become autonomous, adult, responsible. To live is to choose. It is through the making of successive and resolute choices that man traces out his life. Becoming adult is the whole programme of the Freudians, and their work has done much to help us to see its full significance. They stressed first the passage from infantile to adult sexuality and then the passage from captive to oblative love;[1] and lastly the idea of autonomy, the courage to be oneself, in harmony with oneself, to break free from infantile dependence on others.

A young student came to see me. He too had hesitated between his mother and his fiancée. In spite of misgivings, he had given up seeing his fiancée, or at least had only seen her in secret, in order to appease his mother; and since that time he had suffered from all kinds of odd illnesses.

'Is that your aim in life', I asked him, 'to live for your mother?'

Several months later he wrote to me saying that that simple question had set going a complete transformation within him. Once he showed himself firmly resolved, his mother accepted his fiancée perfectly willingly. People who complain of being thwarted have nearly always their own weakness to blame.

[1] René Allendy, *L'amour*, Denoël, Paris, 1942.

I do not wish the reader to misunderstand me. I am not setting young people against their parents, or inciting them to disregard parental advice. Let them follow it provided they are convinced that it is their duty to do so, or even that it is their duty to please their parents. The negation of life is to act against one's better judgment through weakness, because one does not dare to take the responsibility for one's decisions.

Prolonged indecision is a poison as far as the person is concerned. It always arises from some inner conflict which one has not had the courage to resolve, or even to become aware of. It is common among those who have been kept in a state of dependence by domineering parents. It can persist throughout life long after the death of the parents. Such people will tell us quite openly that they do not even know what their tastes, their beliefs, and their aim in life are. As soon as they have made a decision they begin wondering if they have not made a mistake. If we run away from the first choices we are faced with, we sink into a twilight in which we no longer see clearly the decisions that have to be made.

These people are quite content that we should make the choice for them. They ask for advice, for a medical verdict that will protect them from responsibility. This would put an end to their indecision, but it would not solve their problem for them. They would still be children, still constantly in need of us, still dependent. The doctor must be on his guard: he is used to giving orders—that is his role in technical medicine. He often has himself a 'paternal complex' since, like a father with his children, he wants to decide everything for the good of his patient. He even decides sometimes on an operation without taking proper care to make sure that the patient freely consents to it.

This is what Pope Pius XII had in mind when, in a speech to a gathering of neurologists, he solemnly recalled 'the right of the individual to self-determination... the rights of the individual over his own body and life, his bodily and psychological integrity.'[1]

[1] H. H. Pius XII, Allocution to the first International Congress on the Histopathology of the Nervous System, *Acta Apostolicae Sedis*, Rome, 1952.

I have already referred elsewhere to the important inquiry into this subject made by Emmanuel Mounier, the results of which he published in the review *Esprit*.[1] Dr Raymond Trotot, a neuro-surgeon working in Paris, has also expressed himself unambiguously on the matter: 'The domain of the person is inviolable as long as it remains intact, and any intervention in it must only be made with the express consent of the patient.'[2] Respect for the person includes respect for the right of self-determination, since it is precisely the free and responsible commitment of the self which creates the person. 'Person is synonymous with liberty,'[3] writes Professor Hauter. That is why the psychotherapy of the person is, in Dr Roger Reyss-Brion's phrase, a 'non-directive psychotherapy'.

So, even in technical medicine, when we have to make decisions about a course of treatment, our concern for the person obliges us to take the patient into our confidence, so that he can share in the decisions through his freely given consent, knowing what is entailed. But when we come to the medicine of the person, when the patient must choose what course he is to adopt for his life, this concern imposes an even greater reserve upon us: we must help him to make his own decisions, and not make them for him.

Trust is a factor of prime importance; we must trust absolutely his responsible choice, even if it seems to us to be questionable. When the patient's parents—or his brother, his sister, his school-teacher, or whoever it may have been—have been deciding everything for him, even with the best of intentions, in his own interest, they have showed him in so doing that they did not trust his judgment. They have thus sown in his heart that lack of self-confidence which has made him weak, incapable of decision, less than adult, which has hindered the full development of the person in him.

[1] Paul Tournier, *A Doctor's Casebook*, translated by Edwin Hudson, S.C.M. Press, London, 1954, p.49.

[2] Raymond Trotot, *La neuro-chirurgie et la personne humaine*, Médecine de France, Paris, 1954.

[3] *Loc. cit.*

The task of the doctor is to help each of his patients to become a person, to assume his proper responsibilities. Nor does this mean leaving the patient to sort things out entirely by himself, remaining silent through fear that to reveal our own opinion may influence him. A responsible choice is not a blind choice, made in ignorance of the dangers involved in it, and of all the aspects of the problem on which the doctor's experience may be able to throw light.

We come back here to the fundamental notion of the dialogue: that we must say all that we have to say, with complete frankness, but in such a spirit that the person to whom we say it feels that we are doing so only in order to help him to choose his line of action in full awareness of the issues at stake, and that we are prepared to trust his choice even if it is not the one we should make ourselves.

Dr Gerrit van Balen once wrote to me about his concern at how few people today have a real sense of responsibility. I quoted his opinion in the course of a speech I made at a village meeting. The mayor was present, along with several members of the municipal council. One of them got up.

'You remember what we were discussing at the last council meeting', he said; 'we all knew, really, the decision we ought to make. But we referred the matter to the cantonal government so as to avoid taking responsibility for it.'

That does not happen only at municipal council level. It happens at every stage of the political, professional and social hierarchy. From the husband who throws all the responsibility for the household on to his wife, through workmen, foremen, civil servants and heads of departments, right up to the chief ministers who throw their responsibilities on to parliament, how many people there are whose constant concern is to shelter under the authority of others! When an employee is dismissed, what often hurts him most is that his chief has not informed him of the fact directly, but has done it through some underling. Everyone tries to excuse himself by putting the responsibility on to someone else, or by invoking 'bad luck'.

How many people there are who ask everybody's advice, when in reality their mind is already made up, and all they want is to share the risks attendant upon their decision! Is not Sartre right when he says that we choose our advisers according to the advice we expect to receive from them? A man in the throes of a marital conflict, if he inclines towards divorce, will readily consult a psychiatrist who is himself divorced and who may well say to him: 'There are moments in our lives when we must have the courage to look a situation in the face, to admit that what is lost is lost, instead of going on indefinitely weighed down by a mortgage from the past.' If, however, he means to hold on, he will consult a psychiatrist who knows that true courage consists not in flight, but in standing and facing the problems of life.

That is why the psychotherapist, like Socrates, often answers one question with other:

'Do you think I ought to tell my wife?' I am asked by a husband who has just confessed to me that he has been unfaithful to her.

'What do you think yourself?'

It takes plenty of courage to live according to one's convictions. That is why it is always so difficult to break away from social conformity, to act differently from everybody else. And it is because everybody conforms to the 'done thing' that it becomes so hard to depart from it. Thus society becomes a game of personages. 'Dare to detach yourself from the herd,' once wrote Romain Rolland. As soon as a man obeys his inner call, he upsets the game, and brings to light around him the persons buried underneath the personages. Albert Camus gives a penetrating study of this in his book *The Rebel*.[1]

Even the happiest life is a constant struggle to face the problems it raises, the external and internal conflicts it arouses, which are the very stuff of life itself; a struggle to be true to oneself, to

[1] Translated by Anthony Bower and published by Hamish Hamilton, London, 1953.

assume responsibility for one's own convictions and talents. 'It is much easier', I read in a letter from one of my patients, 'to be in the position of a victim than in that of a person conscious of his responsibilities and of the gifts he is endowed with. But it is the only way to inner maturity.'

Then she adds: 'How difficult it is really to accept one's life as it is. But I know that everything comes back to that acceptance —and that it is the real key to happiness.' That is the point— acceptance of one's life has nothing to do with resignation; it does not mean running away from the struggle. On the contrary, it means accepting it as it comes, with all the handicaps of heredity, of suffering, of psychological complexes and injustices.

When the struggle is hard, a sedative, a sleeping-draught, or a rest-cure may procure the necessary relaxation for the battle to be joined anew in better conditions. But they can also be a way of avoiding the struggle. We see here how the perspective of the person obliges us constantly to re-examine the problem of the various courses of action to which technical medicine may point. Surgeons such as Dr William Brunat of Lyons, and Professor Verdan of Lausanne[1] go so far as to say that even proposals for surgical operations must similarly be called in question.

This also goes to show how far the medicine of the person is removed from the sort of sentimentalism which goes soft on the patient. True love of those who come to us is shown in our being filled with ambition for them. It means wanting them to be brave while having ourselves the courage to help them to be so, instead of making ourselves their accomplices in retreat. I was discussing this the other day with a woman patient who was acutely aware of the way in which her life had been gradually impoverished and curtailed by the fear of facing criticism. She felt she was going round in circles, like a horse in a merry-go-round. 'Jump over the hedge, then!'

That is what living means—jumping over the hedges of the personage that have gradually grown up and hemmed us in. It means accepting risks: 'Nothing venture, nothing win,' says the

[1] *Loc. cit.*

proverb. We think that by being cautious we are protecting life, whereas we are slowly smothering it. Our Lord's words come to mind: 'Whosoever will save his life shall lose it' (Mark 8.35). If we hesitate, and retreat when faced with the need to choose, we become, as we have seen, ever more hesitant; we no longer even know what our convictions are. But once we boldly obey the call within us, all these gathering mists are swept away. Life regains its clarity, the person appears, refreshed and able once more to see clearly and to choose.

It has been said that a fruitful life is the realization of an idea. So the person is not a reality given in advance, that can be discovered by objective examination. It is created by a quite subjective decision; it results from a choice. 'I have deliberately preferred', wrote Kierkegaard,[1] 'to use the expression "choose oneself" instead of know oneself.' We can understand now the failure of the intellectualism which claims to know man as an object, a thing.

It is the attitude of the *Journal intime*, like that of André Gide, who refuses to choose in case he makes a miscalculation and amputates something of himself. It was my own attitude in my student days, with the result that I was turning into a dabbler, a dilettante, trying to interest myself in everything. Dialogue with God gave my life an axis. So far from impoverishing it, it has made it more fertile, more interesting, more adventurous.

Choosing also means renouncing. It means defining our person by abandoning resolutely what is not integrated into it by the choice. The intelligence registers everything, turning the person into a kind of limitless museum. It is the will that chooses, and releases the stream of life.

We often see lives that are divided, and paralysed by the division: divided between the dream and the reality, or torn between conflicting centres of interest. There are many men whose hearts are not in their daily work, which has become to them like a ball and chain dragging at their feet. There are large

[1] Søren Kierkegaard, *Either/Or*, Vol. 2, translated by Walter Lowrie, Humphrey Milford, Oxford University Press, London, 1944, p. 216.

numbers of women who are divided between a career and family life. Inevitably, in present-day conditions, there are many women who must go out to work. But even they must make a choice in their own minds about what hierarchy of duties they are to accept.

There are also not a few who live what one might call provisional lives, in which the choice is constantly postponed. Such people's hearts are not in their present lives, for they are always waiting for the time—which never comes—when their true lives will begin. This is often the case with women who want to get married. It is, after all, a very proper desire. But if they live their lives in a state of suspended animation, refusing to take a full part in their existence as it is now, in their life as celibates, they become dried-up and unadventurous, and that very fact diminishes their chances of marriage. And if marriage does not come, they will have spent all their lives just waiting.

Something similar happens in the case of those men (and there are many) who look upon their present occupations as provisional. In such a state of mind they lose all interest and pleasure in their work. Perhaps they go frequently from one provisional employment to another, and their ability to throw themselves heart and soul into the work diminishes daily. I do not say that a man must never change the nature of his employment. But what strikes me is the number of men who have not really chosen the occupations they are in.

Often it has been suggested to them by parents who desired to realize their own ambitions by proxy. Such parents will readily declare that they advised their son because he could not make up his own mind. Here we have a further example of the problem of indecision arising from an inner conflict in the child who is too dependent on his parents. Many others do not even realize that what decided their occupation was a set of circumstances in the face of which they remained entirely passive, so that on their part there was nothing that could be called a choice.

Sometimes a man realizes that his occupation does not fit in with his ambitions, that in fact when he made his choice he had not the courage to take the risks he knew he was called to take. In such a case the rebirth of the person may have to be paid for by a heavy sacrifice of material security. Such an honest choice, however late it comes, is as fruitful as the 'provisional' life is sterile, dragging on from one employment to another with no whole-hearted commitment of the self to any of them. Having a vocation means acting in a spirit of vocation, being convinced that what one is doing is what one is called to do.

But the trouble is that in practice it is not easy to choose between these two roads—between abandoning resolutely one's present life in order to make the life of one's dreams come true, and renouncing the dream in order to throw oneself whole-heartedly into one's present situation. Worst of all is to be unwilling to give up either of them. It is better to make a mistake in an honest choice than never to choose at all.

Let us be honest, however: this theory can lead us into the new dilettantism of imagining that the choice matters little provided we choose! That would be to return to Gide's attitude. A few days ago I was seen by a young woman who longed to make just this affirmation of selfhood that we are discussing. She was reacting against over-cautious parents who, in order to avoid her running risks, exercised a strict control over her.

'We must all experience things for ourselves,' she said.

'Quite!' I replied. 'But all experiences are not equally good.'

Trying everything, choosing indiscriminately under the pretext of assuming one's responsibilities, is not really choosing, nor is it evidence of a responsible attitude, since it is choosing blindly. A true choice necessarily implies reference to a scale of values. It is because he denies all values that Sartre asserts that man finds himself in an agonizing impasse, being forced to choose and yet incapable of choice. It is however worth noting that one cannot read Sartre without realizing that in spite of his theories he still implicitly accepts certain values—coherence of thought, and sincerity towards oneself, for example.

It is quite clear now that the medicine of the person takes us beyond the objective neutrality of the natural sciences, beyond the agnosticism of the pure scientist. This is not to say that it necessarily implies the adoption of the scale of values of the Christian revelation. But it does imply a scale of values of some sort, and therefore a spiritual basis. Underlying every decisive choice there is thus a prior, fundamental choice, a spiritual one, the choice of one's God: what is your God? Your mother, your own self-interest, your instincts, your pleasure, reason, science, or Jesus Christ? Dr Paul Plattner has explained this clearly: 'In purely scientific medicine, there were only causes and effects. Only the cause was known, not the purpose. . . . This is a question which can only be answered by considering things from a spiritual point of view. . . . It is the spiritual factor which gives man his value. . . . Man enters the world of values, the world of aesthetics and of religion, leaving behind him the psycho-somatic world.'[1]

We are not called upon to impose our own scale of values on our patients. But if we help them to recover this fundamental function of life, namely choice, sooner or later they will raise the question of values—the dialogue will become spiritual. I cannot at this point break off the dialogue on the grounds that I am neither a philosopher nor a theologian, but merely a doctor. What I must do then is to know what my own convictions are, and take responsibility for them, without attempting to impose them on others.

I spoke above of the 'becoming adult' of the Freudians. The atheist doctor may well take that as the sole criterion of every choice. But in doing so he is applying a value, something more than a merely naturalist notion. Or, if you will, he is making nature itself a value, a god. Such a doctor, in spite of his claim to spiritual neutrality, is undoubtedly suggesting a value to his patient. He is also putting forward a value in urging his patient to be honest with himself, or when he aims at the Jungian ideal of 'integration', that is to say, the process of becoming aware of one's repressed functions, the acceptance of responsibility for the whole of oneself.

[1] *Op. cit.*

The Christian scale of values, as I have frequently demonstrated already, by no means denies the importance of these ideas advanced by psychology. It contains them, and goes beyond them. To experience the 'new birth' of which our Lord speaks (John 3.3), to become the 'new man' of which St Paul speaks (Eph. 4.24), is indeed to become adult, to attain to the fullness of humanity ordained by God; but it is much more than that. It is to recover, through the redemption of Christ, fellowship with God and dependence on him.

The Bible is the book of choice. From end to end it sets man face to face with the supreme choice which determines all the other choices in his life; from the law of Moses: 'I have set before you life and death . . . therefore choose life' (Deut. 30.19), to the words of Christ: 'No man can serve two masters' (Matt. 6.24). In each of the personal dialogues of which the Bible is full, the Word of God speaks to man, making him a person, a responsible being who must answer. The Bible stresses the inexorable and radical nature of that choice: from the Old Testament, where the prophet Elijah cries: 'How long halt ye between two opinions?' (I Kings 18.21), to the Revelation: 'Thou art neither cold nor hot: I would thou wert cold or hot' (Rev. 3.15).

At the same time, the Bible shows us where true life and liberty are to be found. To see this clearly, take the case of the girl who said to me: 'We must all experience things for ourselves.' She acquiesced at once, her clear eyes looking straight at me, when I answered her: 'But all experiences are not equally good.' She realizes that it is not enough to reject the authority of her parents. That will not nourish life: she must choose another, a truly personal, inspiration. She is oppressed by her parents' domination. To prove to herself that she is no longer a child, she defies it. It is a movement towards liberty, but it is not yet liberty itself.

As long as the children are little, the parents can protect them by their commands. They can forbid them to cross the street alone, for fear of their being run over by a lorry. But the day will come when they must cross it alone, under pain of turning into neurotics, of being crushed, not by the wheels of a lorry, but by neurosis. External protection, therefore, must be replaced by the internal protection of their own judgment, their own personal choice. For there are many lorries on the road of life.

Furthermore, that young woman is profoundly dissatisfied with her career. She was not fond of study, which would have opened the way to other occupations. She would have liked to travel, to broaden the horizons of her experience by visiting other countries. Her parents would not allow her to do this, for fear of the harmful influences under which she might come. And then they wished too to safeguard her material future: 'When one is in a good job like yours, one stays there.'

In order to compensate for her profound dissatisfaction with life she has allowed herself to drift into spending her evenings in a bar with a band of young ne'er-do-wells. As she told me this she was quick to add: 'I don't do anything I shouldn't with them.' This was proof that the question of the choice between good and evil had been raised in her mind. She went on to say at once that she would not have any of them for a husband. In her eyes they were 'just kids'.

'A man for whom a woman is nothing more than a plaything is not at all my ideal,' she said.

But if she was nothing more than a plaything to them, she readily agreed that they were the same for her. It is not with toys that we become adult. What a lot of people there are who content themselves with toys in life—toys that are more or less luxurious, more or less learned, more or less inoffensive. Instead of resolving the problems raised by their dissatisfaction with life, they console themselves with trifling pleasures. Viewed in this light, adultery is seen to be a childish act. Marriage too is a choice, and it is only successful if it involves total commitment. Adultery is an infantile regression; on the one hand, because it is a flight from the responsibilities of this commitment, and on the other because it means treating someone as a plaything.

I have often seen the truth of this in the confessions of a weak man. With his wife he must face the difficulties of mutual adaptation, of the problems of life, of worries over money or the children's education—in short, a dialogue. With the woman he is making love to he has the illusion of a dialogue. Far removed from all the major worries which he forgets in her presence, he finds sweet and flattering consolation. He likes to tell her of all his troubles as a child does to his mother; he presents himself as the victim of circumstances, and awakens the tenderness of her woman's heart. He feels he is understood; he is coddled and consoled; he escapes from conflict. And if occasion arises, he can take a new plaything, as the child who is tired of his own toy covets that of his comrade which seems to him to be much more attractive.

In doing so he thinks he is asserting his freedom, making a spontaneous choice. This is a confusion one often meets with. There are many people who think that being oneself means being spontaneous, that is to say giving way to one's every whim. To act spontaneously is to act without thought, without judgment; it cannot therefore be said to involve choice.

I was talking to a husband about this a few days ago. His wife had been to consult me, and was making a great effort to overcome certain failings of which her husband had complained, and to re-establish harmony between them.

'I recognize that she has changed a lot', the husband told me; 'but it all seems to be lacking in sincerity. She is less natural; she acts as if she were calculating the effect of all she does.'

I explained to him that there are two kinds of sincerity. One is quite natural, and comes during the honeymoon, for instance. The other actually consists in choosing sincerely a specific line of conduct and in keeping to it at the cost of a certain effort of self-control.

This question of spontaneity is an important one. During childhood a man may have undergone some traumatic experience, such as parental domination, or the constraint of an excessively narrow social outlook. He has become caught in the vicious circle of timidity. He shrinks from showing himself as he really is, from letting his true feelings be seen—and even from acknow-ledging them to himself. He must be helped to rediscover his natural spontaneity. The varnish of the personage must be scraped away to reveal once more the true colour of the person underneath. It is a step towards liberty. The current of life begins to flow again.

But this current of life brings with it new problems. He must make a personal choice of the line of conduct he is to follow, decide how he is going to use his new-found liberty. It is then that natural spontaneity is not enough: it would make him an animal, not a person. All sorts of self-betrayals could be justified in its name:

'I cannot help it—I am made that way. People have got to take me as I am,' he might say.

But the truth is that the thing that is going to make a person of him is in some respects the conquering of the instincts of his natural self.

It is here that I part company with my agnostic colleagues who have only a purely naturalistic conception of the evolution of the person, though I admit that I owe a lot to them. For me the person is more than one's nature; it is a supernatural power in us which rules our nature according to the choice it makes. What matters, what makes man a person, is the sincerity of that choice, even if it means, as in the example of which we were speaking, that he must adopt a line of conduct very different from his natural reactions.

Our young woman who wishes to experience things for herself is thus obeying a genuine impulse towards life in seeking to free herself from the domination of her parents. She recognizes too that to act merely out of opposition to them is still not to act freely. And she also sees that to give way to her spontaneous impulses, to choose at random according to the whim of the moment, is only to console herself with playthings. How then is she to become free and living? She is going to come up against a new and more subtle obstacle, that of 'affective transfer'.

She may transfer her feelings of childish dependence from

213

her parents to her doctor. In her mind she may set the doctor over against her parents, leaning on him in order to free herself from them. This will involve a choice, but not a completely responsible one, since she will be seeking to shelter her own responsibility behind that of the doctor. She will follow his example in everything, acting as she thinks he wishes to see her act, espousing his ideas, his philosophy of life, or that which she believes to be his; she will become an ardent propagandist for his psychological theories.

This phenomenon is normal, inevitable and useful, and it is not confined to the psychotherapeutic relationship. When the adolescent begins to call in question the principles passively received from his parents, a friendly elder brother, a schoolmaster, a scoutmaster, or an historical personage such as Socrates, Marcus Aurelius or Pasteur, an author such as Stendhal, Nietzsche or Saint-Exupéry, will exercise a powerful attraction over him. He will wear a Lamartine tie or a Rembrandt hat.

Throughout our lives we model thus our personality physically and morally in imitation of others. As we have seen, we cannot avoid playing a part, adopting a personage of some kind, and it is in the choice of this personage that our person asserts itself. But at the same time this personage limits us, giving rise within us to automatisms which may result in life being stifled, in our freedom of choice being curtailed. This is what happens when the affective transfer is too exclusive and takes on the character of a narrow and prolonged dependence.

At this point any attempt at proselytization on the part of the doctor may bring about in his patient a false conversion, an adhesion to his philosophy, which the patient mistakenly believes to be a free choice on his part. The doctor must efface himself: but behind whom? Behind another man? That would not solve the problem. All human imitation results in a limitation of the patient's horizon. Only God is limitless. The only solution is to respect and encourage the personal dialogue in which the patient engages, often without realizing it, with God himself.

Sometimes, indeed, he thinks he is only talking to himself,

hammering out for himself a philosophy and a morality, helped only by his reason. He may glean elements of it from the writings of the sages of India, of Confucius, Plato or the Stoics, or even in Freudianism, Marxism or Existentialism. In so far as he finds eternal verities in them, he will be piecing together a part of all that is contained in the Christian revelation. He will find in them certain of its principles, such as respect for life, love for one's neighbour, the sense of responsibility, the demand for honesty. So he will be approaching it, as Dr Ramón Rey Ardid says,[1] recalling St Thomas Aquinas' remark: 'Every soul is naturally Christian.' But instead of a living plant, full of rich sap and budding with new shoots, he will only have gathered a bunch of cut flowers, among which, moreover, there is a grave risk of there being some artificial imitations.

However, there is less faith put in reason as a guide for humanity today than was the case in the last century. The atomic bomb has something to do with this. Those scientists who are in the van of scientific progress are themselves afraid of the dangers inherent in it. After having made a public apology to the Japanese people, Professor Robert Moon, one of the nuclear physicists who helped to create the atomic bomb, declared to the Moral Rearmament assembly that this mortal danger would only be removed if we began to listen to what God was saying to us: 'In our time', he added, 'the Holy Spirit must take first place, and the intellect must come second.'

In any case, this gigantic effort to rediscover the great laws of life by means of rational judgment must lead to the turning of them into a rigid morality, a system of abstract principles, like all moralistic systems crushing in its effect. It is not living, but cold and dead. And sooner or later one sees that, in spite of the sincerest of resolves, true fidelity to such principles is impossible. Then there is nothing left but despair or the philosophy of compromises, unless another solution is found, in living fellowship with God: the experience of forgiveness.

It is characteristic of Christianity that choice is made not

[1] *Op. cit.*

215

of principles but of a person, of the living God, of Christ. It does indeed bring with it all the moral principles that can be discovered by reason. But it makes us something more than mere machines applying principles: it makes us persons. It brings us much more than a code of ethics. It brings us a personal relationship, a current of life springing from the very source of all life, and true liberty.

12

NEW LIFE

WHAT CONCLUSIONS are we to draw from our study of the person? We note the remarkably close inter-relation of the ideas of life, liberty and the person. At the beginning of this book I referred to two anniversaries celebrated by my Genevan homeland. Now as I write it is the eve of the first of August, the Swiss national holiday. It is the anniversary of the Grutli Oath, from which was born the Con-federation, which Geneva was the last to enter after having for centuries formed alliances and borne arms in a common cause with many of the Confederate cantons.

On the evening of the first of August the bells will ring out in all the towns and villages of my country, and beacons will be lit on mountain, hilltop and lake-side, recalling the fires that summoned the Confederates to battle in the olden days, in times of danger when the approach of some foreign army threatened their liberties. My homeland has a body: its mountains and valleys, its towns and its countryside; it has a soul—the joys and sufferings of its people, the intelligence of its scholars, the people's tenacious will to work, and their passionate love of liberty.

But my country is more than that; it is a person. The Grutli Oath was an engagement made 'in the name of Almighty God', a solemn choice, a welling up of life which raised that handful of mountaineers out of their miserable condition as distant subjects of the Hapsburgs, to a personal existence. Throughout our history that life has welled up afresh: in the dark hours when it was being stifled amid sterile conflicts or in the narrow conform-ity that settled on the burghers as their prosperity increased, it has been rekindled at the call of inspired men ready to commit themselves boldly and completely.

It is the same with our individual lives. We assert ourselves as persons in the moment of choice freely and responsibly made: then life wells up in us. Thereafter it sinks gradually back into the automatisms it has created and which become our prison. The personage hides the person until it breaks forth once more in a new self-commitment. Life is not a stable state, but a rhythm, an alternation, a succession of new births. We have an image of this in the way its continuity is preserved: it does not go on indefinitely in an unchanging organism, but springs up anew from generation to generation, from birth to birth.

The reader will recall that Claude Bernard distinguished in the living being 'two orders of phenomena': phenomena of life and phenomena of death. The first, he maintained, were internal, silent and hidden. They were inaccessible to scientific observation. They alone were specifically living and creative. We have seen them on the spiritual level, determined by their goal and not by their cause, springing up from contact with others, with our neighbour and with God, through the commitment such contact demands.

The phenomena of death are their visible traces, the automatisms, all that can be objectively observed and studied: the physical reflexes of physiology, the psychical determinisms of scientific psychology. A reflex, however highly evolved, is not an action but a reaction. It is a crystallization of life, surviving in automatism and shorn of every vestige of liberty. We must ask ourselves all the time whether we are really acting, or merely reacting in accordance with the habits we have acquired, whether we are locomotives or waggons, autonomous forces or the passive objects of forces foreign to us, whether we are persons or personages.

True liberty flows, then, from our being freed from automatism. To be free is to become oneself once more, not the biological self of reflexes, of inexorable mechanisms that impede the flow of life, but the self of the person. These moments of liberation are the ones that are truly fruitful. I remember the moment when, suddenly, at the age of thirty-five, I found myself able after a long talk with my wife to weep for the death of my parents whom I had lost when I was still a child. My whole being was shaken to the core, and I felt that an irrevocable change had taken place within me. I was freed from myself, from my personage and from all the unconscious psychological compensations to which the blocking of my emotions had given rise.

How often since then have I seen people going through that same experience in my consulting-room! It is as if a heavy garment were falling away from their shoulders, after having dragged at them and hampered them for so long that they no longer realized that they are restricted by it. That is the aim of the medicine of the person, to allow the person to reappear through a rending apart of the personage. But it is always a rending that hurts, a painful parturition. The personage is powerful, its automatisms hold us, strengthened by their perpetual repetition. When we accuse someone of play-acting, or even of being hysterical, we cannot avoid doing them harm, because we are unjustly suggesting that they could behave differently if they wanted to.

We do not realize how terrible psychological determinism can be. It wears down the will as concrete wears away the finger-nails. A 'complex' is inexorable. On the walls of the fortress a sentry is always on guard, whose name is anxiety. A young woman has suffered grave psychological injury which has set up a barrier against sex. She has an intense longing to discover love, but at the same time she is afraid of it. She happens to go as a delegate to a conference and meets a young man who is attracted by her and pays her an innocent compliment or two. At once the alarm bell is set ringing within her, anxiety, panic is let loose, and she becomes so ill that she has to return home.

This is not confined to the deep-seated complexes that belong to the field of analytical psychology. It is true of all the reflexes that determine our habitual behaviour, constantly governed as it is, without our being aware of the fact, by automatic emotional reactions. Take, for example, the power of jealousy, the action of which can completely override the will, often even to the extent of being quite unconscious.

There is the instinctive jealousy which follows in the footsteps of love as inseparably as a shadow. A woman whose husband has been unfaithful to her again and again undergoes a religious conversion which miraculously delivers her from the violent scenes of jealousy she had been so ashamed of. But then her husband starts yet another amorous adventure; all her old reactions return, and her disappointment is so great that she is brought to the point of doubting her faith.

I must remind her of the power of our nature, which doctors know well—and theologians too, for it was St Thomas Aquinas who said that 'grace does not suppress nature', Grace gives us the victory over our nature; it restores the flow of life which sets us free. But even so, complete freedom will be ours only beyond death and resurrection. And yet a change has taken place in that woman. The proof of this is the fact that she is here in my consulting-room confessing her jealousy and seeking in the fellowship of faith strength to overcome it once more.

A complete and lasting obliteration of reactions that are instinctive and natural to us must always give rise to the suspicion of an unconscious repression rather than the action of grace. I say lasting, because in the first flush of a spiritual experience of this sort we feel as it were delivered from the bondage of both body and mind. But it does not last, and the natural reflexes reappear. If this does not happen, then what has taken place is blocking rather than liberation, repression rather than liquidation. In medical language, we have here the essential mark of the differential diagnosis between the pseudo-solution of pathological reactions and the true solution of grace.

In order to devote myself to the writing of this chapter I have cancelled, for a few days, all appointments with my patients. One young woman reacted with extreme annoyance on being told that I should be unable to see her this week. But I have already had a very good letter from her, in which she asks me to forgive her, and promises to try to help my work rather than hinder it. Her first reaction was a quite natural one; what is supernatural is her letter: she tells me that it was only after praying about it that she decided to write.

Thus it is that the liberty of which we were speaking sometimes comes from a breaking-in of the Spirit which frees us completely from the natural mechanisms by which we have hitherto been determined. But very often we must be content with a more modest liberty: that of recognizing the mechanisms at work so as to conquer them afterwards. Similarly, forgiveness does not mean the conjuring away of the immediate natural reactions of rebellion. It is a second movement which miraculously liquidates the rebellion after it has happened.

The censorship described by Freud, which acts as a barrier to prevent us from becoming conscious of these deep-seated mechanisms, is very strong. The power of overcoming it represents in itself a considerable liberation. And it is at the same time a door that opens on to a wider liberty; for as long as these psychical mechanisms are unconscious they are all-powerful, but when they become conscious they are less so. The way is open then for faith and trust to win their victories.

It is utopian to think that we can live free of all complexes. We are always finding old reactions reappearing in us when we thought we had been freed from them. Living in grace is not the same as living in cotton-wool. He who has tasted grace can no longer be content with compromises, escapism, or psychological compensations. He is constrained to confront all life's problems courageously, and faithfully to do battle with them.

Often, what we believe to be the most characteristically personal thing about us is in reality impersonal, since it is automatic. We are simply the slaves of certain impulses that result from psychological mechanisms entrenched in us by habit. One is a slave to his avarice, another to his prodigality. Both feel uneasy; both have a vague sense of being determined by their complexes, and thus of not being free, of betraying their persons instead of being personal. That this is so is shown by their constant need to reassure and justify themselves. The miser justifies his avarice by criticizing the spendthrift, and the spendthrift justifies his prodigality by criticizing the miser. All systematic criticism of a person or a group of persons is an indication either of jealousy or of some other personal complex.

This is the source of endless marital disputes. For each takes the opportunity of denouncing the failings of the other. The prodigal flatters himself that he is free since he is at liberty to be generous and is not a slave to avarice. And the miser flatters himself he is free since he is at liberty to save money, not being a slave to spendthrift impulses.

This of course applies in every other sphere of life. One is a prisoner of his systematic optimism, another of his systematic pessimism. One is meticulous, another untidy. One is cautious, another bold. One has got into the habit of giving way to his feelings: he is always harping on his own sufferings; he aggravates them by allowing his emotions to take control. Another, on the contrary, always hides his feelings; he bottles them up and suffers more acutely in consequence. One is conventional, another adventurous; one always punctual, another always late. I am waiting for a patient who is making his first visit; he is late. I tell myself that he is perhaps a man who has freed himself from that slavery to the clock which torments so many people. But if he is always late I must think rather that he is not free, and examine with him why that is so.

Constant lateness is not accidental. It may, for instance represent a sort of go-slow strike, a protest against the contingencies of this world, a kind of refusal to accept the conditions of human life and society. Clearly, qualities both good and bad which at first sight appear to be basic to our person, are only secondary characteristics.

To be truly personal is to acquire liberty of conduct, to be, to some extent at least, able to govern oneself instead of being governed by automatisms. It is to be able to be generous or sparing as the changing circumstances require and in accordance with a conviction freely arrived at. It is to be able to be an idealist without losing sight of reality, to be a realist without betraying one's ideals. It is to be orderly without making such a fetish of order that the least disorder is a torture. In the nineteenth century appeal was made to the will. Modern psychology has shown how futile and even harmful is this dependence on our own efforts. All it leads to is the donning of a new artificial personage over the top of the first.

Furthermore, to depend on one's own will-power, one's good resolutions, especially against the impulsions of instinct and the determinism of powerful psychological complexes, is to ask for failure and for a perpetual conflict which will destroy rather than strengthen the forces of the person. It may be successful against a minor failing such as untidiness, but at the price of a new slavery: the slavery of one's own resolutions, which will leave no room for flexibility or for personal fancy. If any unforseen event should happen to upset the established order of things to which one clings, the result will be a state of anxiety.

Does this mean that it is no use trying to exert our wills? By no means. We must apply our efforts at those points where they will be efficacious. I have just been talking to one of my patients who has read my manuscript.

'I was struck by one story', she told me. 'The one about the old spinster who didn't like life. I am the same: I don't like life either—I realize it only too well. I see that it must be a false attitude on my part, but I cannot cure myself of it. Try as I may, I cannot succeed in making myself love life as that old lady did!'

'If you have in your garden an apple-tree that is not bearing fruit', I said, 'you don't accuse it of having a false attitude. Love of life is one of life's natural fruits. Nor do you try to manufacture apples; they have to grow of themselves. What you do is to put all your energies into looking after your apple-tree, manuring the ground, destroying parasites—in short, providing the conditions favourable to its life. The natural sap, the current of life, must be set in motion again.'

True liberation depends, then, on this welling up of life.

That was what happened to the old spinster: her experience of reconciliation with life sprang spontaneously from within, whereas my patient was trying in vain to make it happen. What we can do is to put our whole effort of will into seeking that personal fellowship with God and with our neighbour in which life is renewed and the person is revealed, in which we become conscious of our deepest problems, and in which the breath of the Spirit comes to sweep away like dust the automatisms we had thought to be a part of our person, when they were in reality only a deposit from the past.

Thus two diametrically opposite paths are open to us in our search for liberty—the effort of our own will, which simply means artificially making up a personage for ourselves and achieving a certain skill at the task; and the path of the trusting personal encounter. The first brings tension; the second, an easing of tension. One is a glorification of will-power; the other is self-abandonment. The first is the method of Stoicism; the second is that of modern psychology.

It is a fact that all the schools of psychotherapy encourage and use this trusting relaxation of tension. Whatever the method used—the free association of ideas of the Freudians, the dialogue of the followers of Jung and of Adler, or Desoille's method of the waking dream in which the subject lets his thoughts wander freely and spontaneously in accordance with images suggested to him—the discovery of the person is the result of this abdication of self-constraint.

But this is also the way of Christian faith, which leads man, reconciled to God through Jesus Christ, to a trusting abandonment of himself to him. That is why prayer, and especially common prayer in the community of faith which constitutes the Church, can often have psychological effects very similar to those of a medical cure. In it I can feel that release of new life which renews my entire being, I can discover my person, my true feelings which have been held back or repressed until then, my likes and dislikes, my aspirations, my true convictions.

I see at once how false to myself my habitual way of life has been, even when I have thought I was being sincere. I realize that I have been acting a part, a personage very different from what I really am. Thus laid bare, I find myself again, and at once I experience a tremendous urge to assert myself as I am.

One of my patients is undergoing this moving experience. Suddenly she breaks the silence of her thoughts with a question that has occurred to her:

'But to be myself, assert myself—isn't that just the very opposite of what the Gospel says I must do: deny myself?' (Mark 8.34). She goes on before I can reply, pouring out a flood of childhood memories. She has a sister, and when they were children they often played at wrestling together. The game always ended in the same way, with the victory of her sister, who got her down on to the ground, although the sister was not the stronger of the two.

Children have games like that which always follow the same pattern, like a ceremonial, as if a tacit convention had fixed the way they must end, and the part given to each player. One day, however, without knowing clearly why she did so, my patient had disobeyed the convention, and, using her superior strength, had easily thrown her sister to the ground. The latter had cried out; their parents came on the scene, and the result was that my patient had received a severe scolding for being so naughty to her sister.

Now she realizes that ever since that incident she has in some measure restricted her own life in order not to offend her sister. It was as if the full development of the one depended on the limiting of that of the other. It happens more often than one might suppose. It is particularly common among married couples, one of the partners indulging in self-effacement in order to permit the self-assertion of the other. The result is lamentable—it is no longer a marriage. For marriage ought to mean that each of the partners helps the other to attain fullness of development.

But here everything is false. The one thinks of his self-effacement as being Christian self-abnegation, renunciation of self; while the other becomes tyrannical, taking his despotism for a proper affirmation of self. Indeed, the problem is even more subtle: it often happens that both husband and wife deny themselves all self-affirmation for fear of offending each other, and both are impoverished, since the lives of both are inhibited.

If I were to see my patient's sister, she too would probably discover that she had often held back from asserting herself, out of consideration for her sister. Thus, in countless families and communities, each member appears to be trampled upon by the others, whereas the fact is that each is holding himself in check in the belief that he is thus permitting the full development of the rest.

This is a grave and frequent mistake. To assert oneself, to say what one believes and to act accordingly, is not to offend others, always provided that it is done in charity. Rather does it encourage others to do the same, making possible the authentic dialogue of which we have spoken. And self-renunciation does not in the least mean forcing oneself to put on a self-effacing personage, repressing one's real convictions and pretending to have others which one has not got. It means just the opposite—refusing to invent for oneself a conventional personage, but instead handing over the direction of one's life into God's hands, so that he may awaken our person in accordance with his purpose, in dialogue with him. It means seeking his will, but also daring to assert it.

Many people have a quite negative conception of Christianity, as if it consisted in continual self-amputation, as if God wanted to hold us down, rather than that we should 'turn again and live'. Would such a God deserve the name of Father which Christ gave to him? When I labour to liberate a crushed life, I am not fighting against God, but with him. Like a gardener who removes from around a plant the weeds that choke it, using all the care that as one of God's creatures it deserves, I am helping to re-establish his purpose of life.

It is God who gave it life, and he surely wants it to flourish and bear fruit. Does not Christ often speak of bearing fruit? Bearing fruit means being oneself, asserting oneself, growing in accordance with God's purpose.

Christianity, therefore, has its positive, affirmative, creative aspect—ignored by many Christians. I do not deny that it imposes certain specific acts of renunciation. Jesus spoke of the husband-man who prunes his vine so that it may bear more fruit. The purpose of pruning is not to restrict life, but on the contrary to promote its fuller and richer flow.

Christian life, then, is liberty, the liberation of the person from the trammels imposed by external influences. It is the rising of the sap from within. It is life under God's leadership. It is a balance between prayer and action: between the dialogue in which his creative inspiration is sought, and the bold and confident affirmation of self, in which the inspiration received is put into practice. The personage is the prison of automatism, the false renunciation like that of my patient who was restricting her life; the person is a free engagement, the restoration of the divinely-appointed order.

I do not claim that the enterprise is easy. Throughout this book I have tried to show that we never attain complete freedom of the person from the personage. Our dialogue with God is always spasmodic and veiled. But however difficult and in-complete the search for God's guidance, it is nevertheless that which creates the person, that which is the source from which new life and liberty spring.

It is in this attitude, this conversation face to face with God, that the miser can recognize his avarice, and free himself from it instead of trying to justify it; then he can turn towards generosity. The spendthrift, too, can free himself, and administer his goods more wisely. Life is restored to suppleness from the rigidity of automatisms and fixed principles. Seeking God's purpose means whole-heartedly accepting each circumstance that arises, facing all the problems it raises, and listening to what God is saying through it.

To depend on God is to be free of men, things and self. It is to be able to take pleasure in all his gifts, without being the slave of any. It is to be able, as occasion demands, to spend and to save, to speak and to forbear, to act and to rest, to be grave and gay, to defend oneself and to surrender.

There comes to see me an artist who has reached the acme of success. Since his youth he has directed all his energies towards this end, and now he has gained a world-wide reputation.

'From the professional point of view', he tells me, 'I can wish for nothing more. My dreams have come true. But I have come to see you because I feel that I lack something. It gives me no pleasure.'

He explains that his father was a weak sort of man, incapable of defending himself in the struggle for existence. The son, having suffered in childhood from the poverty into which, through no fault of its own, the whole family had been plunged, owing to the father's inability to cope with competition, determined to bend all his will to the struggle for success.

And now that he has obtained it, he is imprisoned by the attitude he adopted. He finds no pleasure in his success, and cannot stop working. He is not happy in his marriage, and realizes that he demands too much of his wife, just as he does of himself.

'The trouble is', I said to him, 'that you can't take things easy, which is very important for an artist.'

'Yes, that's it, I can't relax; I am always at full stretch.'

But where does one draw the line between taking things easy and being lazy? It is in prayer that one is able to see whether the time one 'wastes' is a renunciation, a proper relaxation willed by God, or on the contrary disobedience.

Depending on God involves seeking his will as to how our time should be employed. Dr Théodore Bovet wrote an admirable little book on this subject.[1] In order to find the calm necessary for a more personal medicine, in order to find the time that is indispensable for meditation and for family life, I have had to put

[1] Théodore Bovet, *Zeit haben und frei sein*, Furche Verlag, Hamburg, 1954.

228

off many of my patients, say no to many requests for articles or speeches. I have found it hard to do, for I never like to disappoint people. But is it not just self-conceit, this desire to be appreciated? If I were to say yes to everybody I should not be a free agent, a person, but the slave of the 'race against time' which is one of the curses of the modern world.

I have been talking to a man in his forties, who is trying honestly to draw up the balance-sheet of his life. He has been in all sorts of jobs, moved from one position to another, never satisfied. He has known several women, but been unable to become really attached to any. People say he is easy-going and unadaptable. It is true, but not the whole truth. He explains that he has always been in search of the Absolute, that he has sought it everywhere. He cannot put up with evil. When an employer or an overseer treats him harshly, he is annoyed and discouraged. He takes himself off without a word, to continue his search elsewhere.

I can sympathize with that man. I feel myself close to him. I too, passionately seek the Absolute. But the absolute he is looking for is a fairy-tale absolute; a complete and unblemished absolute in which he can take refuge without fear of disappointment or limitation. And now he contemplates the poverty of his life. He has run away from the difficulties instead of facing them. He has always broken off the dialogue in which the person is forged. And his person, instead of developing, has dwindled. He no longer knows even what he wants; he is becoming incapable of choosing, of taking on any responsibility; his life is slipping away between his fingers.

Plenty of people tell him that there is no such thing as an Absolute, that all he can hope for is an occasional and passing enjoyment, if he is to possess anything at all. This makeshift philosophy cannot satisfy him. But I know that the Absolute does exist, that it can be tasted and handled. If one cannot possess it, one can experience it, see it revealed, in those brief moments when life, absolute life, wells up. It is not a state, but a movement, a trembling, a thrusting forward, which happens just at the culminating point of the struggle which is forced upon us by evil without and within, the world outside that has to be faced and our own interior world.

Claude Bernard used to describe life as a conflict between the organism and its environment. And it is precisely because the world is relative, imperfect, incomplete like ourselves—that new life is always springing up amidst the resultant conflicts. A completely satisfied man would be a fossil. Dissatisfaction maintains the constant movement of life, like an unending search. 'Men seek the chase, and not the quarry,' wrote Pascal. The Absolute is in this search itself. The Absolute is not of the order of things, not even absolute, perfect things; it is of the order of persons, and of their revolt against the imperfection of things.

Life is not a state, it is a movement. Nowhere in nature does it present the character of a fixed and stable maximum, but rather of an undulation, successive waves of life. Sincerity, as we have seen, is not a perfected state, but a movement experienced just at the point at which one perceives that one lacks it. Love is not a state, it is a movement. Personal contact is not a state, but a fleeting movement that must be ceaselessly rediscovered. Marriage is not a state, but a movement—a boundless adventure.

Nor is spiritual life a state. Faith is a movement towards God, a turning back towards God which one feels at the very moment when one confesses that one has turned away. That is why Jesus Christ compared the spirit to the wind, of which one does not know 'whence it cometh, and whither it goeth', to a force that passes, which cannot be laid hold of by the hands, and yet which quenches our thirst for the Absolute.

The person too is something that is uncompleted and evades our grasp. It imparts movement to our being, always refashioning our body and soul. The flowering of the person is not a state at which we arrive, it is the movement that results from perpetual incompleteness. If that flowering were the final stage of development, it would be also the halting of life. The rose that is in full bloom is already begining to fade. Nor is the blossoming of the person, as so many people think, an accumulation of knowledge and experience, as it were stones placed one upon another to form a monument. The only result of that would be a grandiose personage, not a person.

The person belongs to the realm of quality, not quantity. It is suddenly manifested in a powerful inner movement which partakes of the nature of the Absolute. However many things we accumulated, that would bring us no nearer to it. The person resides in being, not in having. It is beyond all measure; it eludes every test; it is outside all definitions. The claim to self-knowledge is the surest road to a misunderstanding of self.

Thus the infirm, the neurotic, the aged, can experience this flowering of the person, in spite of all that hinders and limits their existence, much more intensely, sometimes, than those who are loaded with the good things of life. Dr Brunat of Lyons once spoke to me of his fear that people might be led astray by a false idea of the aims of the medicine of the person; that they might pursue the dream of a glorification of man, of his quantitative development: the dream of a life without limitations and suffering. Much that has been written by psychologists is calculated to cause confusion of this sort; as if human fulfilment depended on the solution of every problem and the removal of every limitation.

The person is something very different from a nice, round fully-inflated balloon. Rather is it an imponderable, an inner experience which can take place in sickness as well as in health. It is a germ that develops. What is a grain of wheat? You have not defined it when you have weighed it, measured it, and submitted it to chemical analysis and microscopic examination. It contains a whole plant which you cannot yet see. What is a silkworm? You cannot define it without seeing in advance all its metamorphosis. What is a child? You cannot describe him without thinking of the whole life of the man, with all its unknowns, for which he is preparing.

We have been brought to an open, rather than a closed, notion of the person, like the distinction which Bergson made between open and closed minds. Closed minds are dead minds, just as the ready-made absolute of the fairy-tale, which the man I was speaking of just now was looking for, was a dead absolute, not a living one. We must resist the temptation to give a doctrinaire answer to the question with which we began this book: 'Who am I?' We must give up the idea that knowing the person means compiling a precise and exhaustive inventory of it. There is always some mystery remaining, arising from the very fact that the person is alive. We can never know what new upsurge of life may transfigure it tomorrow.

The person is a potential, a current of life which surges up continually, and which manifests itself in a fresh light at every new blossoming forth of life. At the creative moment of dialogue with God or with another person, I in fact experience a double certainty: that of 'discovering' myself, and also that of 'changing'. I find myself to be different from what I thought I was. From that moment I am different from what I was before. And yet at the same time I am certain that I am the same person, that it is the very same life which is thus welling up anew, that it was contained in my being as it was yesterday, even though then there was nothing that could lead me to suspect what I am discovering today.

We never have more strongly the impression of personal life, of self-discovery, than in that moment when we feel ourselves going beyond ourselves, carried along by a force which comes not from us, but from God. The shape of our whole life is about to be altered, and yet it is at that instant that our authentic person has been awakened in that upsurge of life. That moment may contain the germ of a whole life-work. That is what happened in the case of the philosopher Charles Secrétan. He describes movingly how, as a youth, he stood on the roof of the church at Montreux looking out over the splendid scenery of Lake Leman, and suddenly realized how great God is. It was a moment of true fellowship with God, of dialogue with him, which contained within it the whole of his philosophy of liberty, which was to be his life's work.

But that is not a privilege confined to a few exceptional thinkers. It is the normal process of the development of the person. It is not continuous, but intermittent. We cannot manufacture it; all we can do is to prepare the way and the climate for it. It springs up of itself, just as in physical medicine we do not manufacture life, but simply create the conditions that are favourable to it.

We can help our patients by all the physical and psychological means at our disposal. But the essential aid, that which touches the person, its awakening and growth, can come only from God. Faith consists in this waiting upon God's intervention, which resolves what we are incapable of resolving.

With a patient we work for weeks—even months—on end, in utter darkness, and suddenly a light shines—not from us—to illuminate that life. During all the time we have been concerning ourselves with our patient's body and mind, helped by the personal contact established between us another dialogue has been going on in the darkness. The living God has been breaking in upon that person, rousing into activity the guiding force which will suddenly manifest itself in a free and responsible engagement in which the stake is nothing less than the patient's destiny itself.

Taking up an analogy which we have used before, and which we can now complete, our life is a score composed by God. The person is the conductor who is assuring its performance by directing the orchestra—our body and mind. But the composer is not absent. He is there during the performance. He leans over to the conductor and encourages him; he whispers in his ear, making clear his intentions and helping him to put them into execution.

So our person is, as it were, bound up with our destiny. Something of it is revealed at every turning-point in our lives, whether the turning be important in itself or not. But to the end the revelation remains incomplete. The person is still unseen; what we see is but the reflections of it in the manifestations of the body and the mind. It eludes all our attempts to lay hold on it in order to dissect it. The more knowledgeable we are, the greater is the risk of misunderstanding it.

It is a mysterious spiritual reality, mysteriously linked to God, mysteriously linked with our fellows. We are aware of these links at those privileged moments when there springs up a fresh current of life, bursting the fatal fetters of the personage, assserting its freedom and breaking out into love.

INDEX

Adler, 22, 57, 224
Adolescence, 69-70, 118, 126
Adultery, 211
Allendy, R., 32, 200
Amiel, H. F., 68, 69
Archetypes, 55, 58, 71, 73, 97, 113
Art, 114, 123, 179
Asceticism, 118
Atomic bomb, 215
Atonement, 171
Avarice, 221-2, 227

Baruk, H., 60, 174
Baudouin, C., 62
Bergson, H., 100, 151, 231
Bernard, C., 85, 88-9, 92, 94, 99, 103, 218, 230
Bernard, St, 117
Bible, 76-7, 103, 116, 118, 132, 133, 162-5, 167, 169, 170, 172, 175, 199, 210
Bindschedler, J.-D., 163
Boehme, 79
Bovet, T., 35, 228
Brunat, W., 205, 231
Buber, M., 129
Buffon, 79

Calvin, Calvinism, 30, 150
Camus, A., 204
Carrel, A., 186
Caruso, I., 109
Catharsis, 110, 128
Celibacy, 55, 139-40
Cervantes, 13
Chesterton, G. K., 182
Choice, 90-1, 94-5, 98, 101, 127-30, 133, 138, 171, ch. 11, 229
Church, 116, 117, 155-7, 173, 194, 224
Claudel, P., 68

Confession, 155-8, 159, 160, 162, 174, 192
Confucius, 100, 215
Conversion, 162
Corot, 100
Cossa, P., 96

Death, 27, 43, 49, 75, 76, 88, 92, 97, 99, 109, 153, 161, 218, 219, 220
Delay, J., 186
Descartes, 85, 124
Desoille, 224
Determinism and free will, 26
Dialogue, 127-46, 148, 153-4, 156, ch. 9, 182, 184, 188, 189, 191, 193-7, 203, 206, 209, 212, 214, 224, 226-7, 232
Diaries, 68-70, 126, 168
Divorce, 108, 116, 204
Dreams, 25, 47, 56-7, 59-60, 62, 73, 76, 82, 109, 162, 206, 208
Drever, J., 113n.
Dubois, Dr, 135, 157
Ducatillon, Père, 155
Duhamel, G., 185
Durand, Dr, 157

Economics, 180
Einstein, 85
Ellul, J., 171
Epidaurus, 132
Escalade, 11, 20
Evolution 94
Existentialism, 49, 215

Fall, the, 76
Fashion, 79
Flue, N. de, 20
Forel, O., 149
Forgiveness, 38, 98, 115, 215, 221

Index

Francis de Sales, St, 69
Francis of Assisi, St, 115, 117, 182-3
Freud, S., Freudians, 22, 23, 50, 57-9, 63, 71, 73, 109, 111, 113, 114, 128, 134, 157, 200, 209, 215, 224
Friedel, J., 86

Georgi, F., 105
Gide, A., 68, 69, 206, 208
Glossolalia, 173
Gonseth, F., 26, 184
Gosse, Sir E., 125
Green, Julien, 68
Guilt, sense of, 50, 112, 155
Gusdorf, G., 58, 67, 69, 73n., 100, 130n.
Guye, Ch.-E., 86n., 87

Habit, 51-2, 98, 151, 218, 221
Handwriting, 80
Haste, 145, 147
Hate, 54
Hauter, C., 188, 202
Health, 200
Heisenberg, 85
Hinduism, 114
Hippocrates, 104, 132
History, 11, 20, 24, 93, 162, 187
Holy Spirit, 163, 169, 194, 215, 224
Huebschmann, H., 107
Humanism, 158
Humour, 144, 146
Hypnosis, 126
Hypochondria, 96
Hysteria, 219

Id, 175
Impotence, 59
Indeterminacy, principle of, 85
Inferiority complex, 51, 58

Jealousy, 220, 222, 226-7, 230
Jesus Christ, 19, 38, 115, 116, 118, 132, 133, 160, 163, 171-3, 175, 192, 197, 206, 209, 210, 224

Jung, C. G., Jungians, 13, 22, 23, 58, 59, 61-3, 69, 71, 73, 97, 112, 209, 224

Kierkegaard, S., 206
Kretschmer, 104
Kütemeyer, 111

Language, 30, 173
Lateness, 222
Lavoisier, 85
Lawrence, Brother, 183
Laziness, 196, 228
Leriche, R., 106
Life, 29, 32, 33, ch. 5, 102, 103, 112, 114-16, 118-19, 161, 172, 173-4, 175, 181, 195, ch. 11, ch. 12

Mach, R.-S., 43, 186
Maeder, A., 110, 111, 113n., 128, 134, 161, 168, 189
Man, unity of, 15, 26
Marcel, G., 32
Marriage, 16, 34-5, 110, 134, 136-40, 146, 152, 154, 199, 207, 211, 225-6, 230
Marxism, 215
Maternal instinct, 98
Mauriac, F., 68, 169
Mechanization of life, 39-45, 158
Medicine, impersonality of, 43, 185
Medicine of the person, 43-5, 185-90, 192-3, 202, 208, 219, 228, 231
Memory, 70, 87, 91, 94, 127, 155
Menkès, G., 105n.
Mental sickness, 152
Michelet, 157
Mind, 103-5, 107, 108, 109, 111, 112, 124, 129, 157, 163, 169, 180, 187, 220
Mitscherlich, A., 113
Modesty, meaning of, 138
Montaigne, 67, 68
Moon, R., 215
Mounier, E., 202
Music, 133
Myth, 132, 133

Napoleon, 80
Nature, laws of, 85-6
Nédoncelle, M., 188
Neubauer, V., 186
Neurosis, 195-6, 211, 231
New birth, 210, 218
Newton, 85
Nietzsche, 69, 108
Noüy, Lecomte du, 87, 89
Nudism, 76

Obsession, 82
Ochsenbein, H., 172
Odier, C., 113
Optimism, 222
Orelli, A. von, 129, 161, 175, 179
Organic sensitivity, 91, 93, 106
Ors, E. d', 169

Pascal, 31, 33, 51, 123, 172, 230
Patriotism, 17, 19, 217
Paul, St, 54, 76, 83, 103, 116, 133,
    165, 175, 210
Pavlov, 22, 26, 113
Personality, 79, 112-13
Pessimism, 222
Pharisees, 118, 175
Pictet, R., 84, 85
Pindar, 81
Pirandello, 13
Pius XII, 201
Plato, 133, 215
Poetry, 74, 75, 133, 143, 183
Poincaré, H., 85
Ponsoye, P., 101
Prayer, 35, 108, 116, 117, 160, 166,
    168-70, 173, 176, 189, 192, 221, 227
Professionalism, 36-7
Psychiatry, 104, 152
Psychoanalysis, 26, 30, 56-7, 60-3,
    73, 82, 134, 196, 219
Psychological tests, 41, 112
Psychology, 22-3, 24, 37, 41, 50, 51,
    57-8, 61-3, 86, 97, 99, 107, 108,
    109, 111-14, 118-19, 146, 157, 170,

175, 179, 180, 193, 195-7, 205, 210,
    214, 218, 223, 231, 233
Psychotherapy, 45, 61, 105, 109, 110,
    111, 118, 127-8, 132, 134, 135, 157,
    159, 164, 168, 192, 193, 195, 202

Rank, 111
Reason, 55, 74, 75, 215-16
Relativity, 85
Renan, 86
Repentance, 115, 174
Responsibility, 128-9, 157-8, 161,
    171, ch. 11, 218
Resurrection, 220
Rey Ardid, R., 189, 215
Reyss-Brion, R., 202
Rolland, R., 204
Romains, J., 42, 148
Rorschach test, 112
Rostand, J., 26, 86, 87, 90
Rougemont, J. de, 90, 91, 142
Rousseau, J.-J., 20, 67
Rouvière, H., 101

Saint-Exupéry, A. de, 182
Salvation, 111
Sarradon, A., 78
Sartre, J.-P., 32, 49, 50, 130, 171, 204,
    208
School, 19, 33, 132, 133
Science, 13, 23, 41, 43, 62, ch. 5, 102,
    109, 112, 119, 123, 124, 129, 132,
    135, 192, 208-9, 215, 218
Secrétan, C., 232
Secrets, 125-8, 138-9, 150-1, 155, 159,
    181
Self, understanding of, 14, 36, ch. 3,
    67-73, 75, 83
Sex, 35, 53, 58-9, 63, 98, 110, 138-40,
    200, 219
Shri Ramakrishna, 71
Siebeck, R., 40, 86, 174, 189-90
Sin, 60, 109, 110, 114, 155, 174
Sincerity, need for, 12, 21-2, 24, 72,
    115, 154, 157, 159, 165, 213

Index

Social conventions, 18, 28-33, 73-5, 77, 79, 148, 204
Social insurance, 44
Sociology, 180
Socrates, 67, 133, 186
Sonderegger, Dr, 157
Sophocles, 13
Soul, 111, 112, 160, 163
Soul-healing, 109-10, 159
Specialization, 43-4, 180, 185-7
State vs. individual, 40-1
Stocker, A., 111, 156, 161
Stoics, 214, 224
Suggestion, power of, 50-1
Surgery, 60, 78, 111, 205
Szondi's tests, 112

Tears, 75
Tell, William, 11, 20
Ten Kate, J., 123
Thomas Aquinas, St, 215, 220
Thurian, M., 156

Tradition, 11, 20, 75
Transference, 110, 128, 213
Travel, meaning of, 132
Troisfontaines, R., 27
Trotot, R., 202
Tuberculosis, 107-9, 195
Tzanck, A., 86, 88, 91, 94, 95, 98-9, 103

van Balen, G., 195, 203
van den Berg, Professor, 123-4
van Loon, Dr, 164
Verdan, C., 185, 205
Vernet, M., 90-1, 115
Vincent, A., 189
Vital force, 89, 103
Vocation, 82, 169, 174, 176 208

Weisberger, Dom, 169
Weizsäcker, V. von, 86, 113
Wesley, C., 117